The Higaonon Ethnohistory of Rogongon, Lanao del Norte

The Higaonon Ethnohistory of Rogongon, Lanao del Norte

Ma. Cecilia B. Tangian, Ph.D.

To order additional copies of this book, contact:
Xlibris Corporation
1-888-795-4274
www.Xlibris.com
Orders@Xlibris.com
91756

CONTENTS

CHAPTER 1

The Higaonon Tribal Identity

The Higaonon of Mindanao belonged to the original stock of proto-Philippine or proto-Austronesian who came from South China thousands of years ago earlier than the Ifugao and other terrace-building people of Luzon (Elkins, 1996). In Mindanao, the Higaonon tribe settled in Rogongon at the Northern and Central sections of Lanao del Norte. Rogongon is a community of varied cultures known to be the melting pot of the tri-people of Mindanao: the Christian, the Muslim and the Higaonon Filipinos.

The Higaonons in Lanao del Norte are one of the least identified Indigenous group in the area due to its diminishing population. One reason is attributed to intermarriages of the Higaonon to that of the lowland Christians and the Kolibugan indigenous group. Thus, the social interaction produces another dimension of cultural change such as the religious upheaval due to the transformation of the Higaonon's nature belief system to Christianity or Islam.

This book narrates the Higaonon ethnohistory and it analyzes the social and cultural transformation of the tribal group with imphasis on their traditional belief system in terms of their adherence to nature worship; its myth, legend, and epic that embody their traditional belief system; its landmarks and sites considered to be sacred in the context of their traditional beliefs; its social conditions and the social factors which contributed to the changes of the Higaonon traditional beliefs. Oral history gathered from the forty-two (42) key informants consisted of datus, baylans, barangay officials and senior citizens. The data taken from the secondary sources were also considered. The government reports under the National Commission on Indigenous People regarding their customary laws were carefully examined. The data from the National Statistics Office regarding population and the Higaonon settlement was used. These sources were evaluated to corroborate the testimonies given by the key informants. Aside from the government reports secondary materials and reference were given importance. The publication of various anthropological books and the issue of Episcopal Commission on Interreligious Dialogue were taken. Ultimately, the descriptive survey of Rogongon as a place of study was thoroughly conducted for a period of five (5) months.

The Philippine National Historical Institute (PNHI) identified its focus on local studies to enable the people to understand the grassroots of Filipino civilization and mass culture. Ethnohistory is not an exemption to this. Gloria (1987) published works on Bagobo Ethnohistory of Davao. She stressed the need of writing their beliefs using oral interview. Bauzon (1980) on the other hand, emphasized on the value of local history in shedding light on the values, attitudes and experiences of the masses of Filipino society, as well as on the process of social change affecting them in the context of Philippine cultural tradition. Corollary to this concept, this study analyzed the traditional beliefs of the Higaonons in view of their values, attitudes and practices within their respective community, with emphasis on their views and responses to the inroads of Spanish civilization in the sixteenth century and the dynamics of westernization in the nineteenth century. Mojares (1980) proclaimed that there is an inevitable need on the explorations of rural history in the regional, provincial and municipal level in reference to folk or peasant histories. In the light of this research work, the author endeavors to delve into the innate characteristics of this tribe in account of their folkways and traditional beliefs. On this score, the need to understand these people in preserving their culture and tradition is of paramount importance. In this respect, we are building the historical scholarship not only with the general framework of the influential people in history but also on the account of the Higaonon practices whose indigenous culture is still practiced despite the advent of western civilization.

The study has unraveled the historical accounts on the basis of the Higaonon traditional beliefs. It strengthened the foundations of their respect to superbeing, the lesser beings, the elementals and spirits of their dead ancestors. Furthermore, this study accounts the Ethnohistory of the Higaonon in Rogongon specifically on the continuity and change of their traditional beliefs.

Conceptual Framework

According to Gloria historical event should be directly proportional to that of the historical impact, this means that the development of culture reflects dynamism, patterns of interaction that has taken place between and among the cultural subsystems of ideology, social organization and personality. Thus, historical events as an evolutionary process may be said to exert a random and differential response from individuals depending upon the degree of impact.

She further stated that ethnohistory of a certain tribal group proceeds from a developmental understanding of history. Culture changes over time and therefore, has history. The historical process itself is a succession of historical events, both natural as well as social have an impact on people and societies. Mercado (1998) classified indigenous people's communities as culturally and socially distinct from the mainstream societies. The tribal community of Rogongon has a distinct cultural system from other barangays in Iligan, Lanao del Norte. This is due to their adherence and preservation of traditional beliefs that influence their way of life making them a distinct tribe. Gottschalk (1969) stressed his pluralist school of historical causation in explaining certain phenomenal conditions over a certain period of time. As a pluralist he stated that there are several acceptable orderings of history in the explanation of event. The Higaonons in Rogongon had its cause and effect that can be classified into social and cultural phenomena. Contemporary Filipino historians like Agoncillo (1990) are more inclined towards a pluralistic interpretation of cause rather than the listing of the chronology of events. He described the motives and forces behind the events of a historical phenomenon as the subject of study.

The National Commission on Indigenous Peoples also known as NCIP under the Republic Act No. 8371 is instrumental in the recognition, protection and promotion of the Higaonons' rights and privileges towards the practice of their traditional beliefs. In this regard, the Higaonons would better appreciate their own culture. The idea of peace among the Higaonons could be achieved through attending conference regarding Indigenous People Belief System.

Moreover, the Presidential Adviser for Peace Process (OPAPP) with the Episcopal Commission on Interreligious Dialogue (ECID) conducted seminars and series of conference to institute measures in breaking cultural differences and ideologies thereby promoting peace. The agency focuses on a solution for the attainment of peace in Mindanao and in the Higaonon community in particular

CHAPTER 2

Traditional Belief System of the Higaonon

The Tabular representation showing the Traditional Belief System

Superbeing and the Lesser beings	Beliefs
A. Superbeing "*magbabaya*"	The role protector Creator of the universe, and Supreme god of the Higaonons in Rogongon
Lesser Beings "*diwatas*"	
Pinag-aso	Protector of animals, fouls and livestocks
Bulalakaw or "*tagabusay*"	Protector of all water formations
Amomogpog	In-charge of the egg breaking ceremony
Ananaplid or kahungko sa lasang	He owns the *gantangan pandaut sulutan*
Tagabalite	Protector of the forest and *balite trees*
Ananampoc	In-charge of the rattan for cutting feuds
Tagabato	Protector of the rocks
Tagabito	Protector of the caves
Tagaabaga	Protector of the waterfalls
Tagaliyang	Protector of the interior of the cave
Ibabasuk or Tagabugta	Protector of the farmlands and agriculture

B. Elementals "dili ingon nato"	
Good elementals or "diwatas"	guide or abay of the baylans help restore illness due to buyag
Bad elementals or "padedeng"	harm the bypassers like in the balite and kantil can cause ailments like headache and vomiting due to buyag
C. Spirits of the dead ancestors or "*gimukod*"	Joins the magbabaya Act as manlulunda or right hand of magbabaya
Apo Sominam-ang kon Tominokol	Protector of Limunsudan falls
Apo Nangadun	Takes care of good health
Apo Pamamahandi a tolon	Takes care of wealth such as puthaw or metal
Apo Palatambul so Palakampana	Takes care of sounds
Apo Pamulaw	Takes care of the calamities like drought
Apo Pinighawan	Takes care of the betel nuts as ritual component
Apo Dalinason	In charge of the power of the baylans as healers
Apo Magbabasuk	in charge of farming activity
Apo Mangawan	takes care of the mountainous and sacred sites
D. Inanimate objects "balaang butang"	
Gantangan pandaut sulutan	Symbolizes the Higaonon system of justice
Bangkaw and pahawan	Used for hunting purposes
Salikot, kalasag and tango	Sharp weapons for hunting purposes
Kaban and tibud	Depository items on jewelries and clothes
yahong	Container used for ritual

Superbeing known as "magababaya" and lesser beings known as "diwatas"

The Higaonons in Rogongon claimed that they call their Superbeing as *magbabaya*. He is the sole protector, creator of the Universe and the Supreme. Basadre (1998), in her Ethnographic study of the Manobo in Bukidnon accounts that the Manobo called their supreme god as *magvavaya*. Igsolin who was a Manobo shared during the Conference on Indigenous People Belief System at Samal Island on July 2000. He said that *magvavaya* of the Manobos and the *Magbabaya* of the Higaonons are the same. That is, similar to that of the Higaonon *Magbabaya*. Bae Emahan Pianza, shared that the Hiagonons respect nature with reverence because *"kanang kinaiyahan maoy hinimo sa magbabaya nga labawng makagagahum sama sa bukid, bungtod, bakilid, kahoy, dagkong bato, suba ug uban pa. Ang matag lakang nga among pagahimoon gagumikan sa pagpangayo ug pananghid gikan sa pwersa sa kinaiyahan nga gibantayan sa mga espiritu nga maoy pagaingnon nga manlulunda"* (nature is god's creation which consist of mountains, hills, valley, trees, rocks, rivers and others. Every action that we execute requires asking permission from the forces of nature guided by the spirits known to us, as the lesser gods). A few of the lesser gods according to Kagawad Diodato Abungan include *"mga manlulunda o mga espiritu mao ang pinag-aso, bulalakaw, tagabusay, tagabalite, tagabato, tagabito, tagaabaga, tagaliyang, tagabugta ug ibabasuk. Si pinag-aso mao ang tigbalantay sa mga hayop, gansa ug mga manok dinhi sa Rogongon. Ang bulalakaw o ang tagabusay mao ang tigbantay sa katubigan sama sa suba ug busay. Ang ibabasuk o ang tagabugta mao ang nagpanalipud sa kaumahan. Ang tagabalite mao ang manalipod sa kalasangan ug kakahuyan. Ang tagabato ang manalipod sa dagkong bato ug ang tagabito mao ang nagbantay sa langub ug ang tagaliyang mao ang nagbantay sa sulod sa langub"* (the spirits are the following: *Pinag-aso, Bulalakaw* and *tagabusay, tagabalite, tagabato, tagabito, tagaabaga, tagabugta* and *ibabasuk. Pinag-aso* serves as the protector of animals, fouls and livestock in Rogongon. The *Bulalakaw* also known as *tagabusay* is the protector of all water formation. *Ibabasuk* also known as *tagabugta* serve as the protector of all farmlands. *Tagabalite* serves as the protector of the forests and trees, *tagabato* protector of rocks, *tagabito* serves as the protector of the caves and *tagaliyang* the protector of the interior of the cave). Inay Edloy So-ong who studied the bible stated that *"Ang manlulunda duna say ranggo nga makumpara sa mga kristyanong santos. Kon para sa mga Kristyano si San Roque nga maoy magbalantay sa iro, si Pinag-aso maoy nagbantay sa kahayopan para kanamong mga Higaonon"* (the lesser gods have the same functions which are comparable with those of the Christian saints. Example is attributed to San Roque of the Christians as the protector of dogs is equivalent to *Pinag-aso* as protector of all animals among the Higaonons). Alvin Cunto mentioned that *"kon ang tawo kinahanglan mutago sa langub, siya gayud maga-obserba sa usa ka ritwal aron sa paglikay sa dautang epekto nga nagagumikan sa tagaliyang ug tagabito. Ang mangangayam moplastar sa paghatag ug mama, sinsilyo, kan-on nga humay ug manok ug usab magasulti kini ug pag-ampo para sa grasya gikan kang magbabaya. Kami magpadayon ug pagpananghid ngadto kang tagaliyang ug tagabito aron matugutan sa pagsulod sa langub"* (when a person intends to take a refuge in a cave, the person has to observe a cave ritual to avoid harmful effects that could be attributed to *tagaliyang* and *tagabito*. The cave ritual is as follows: The hunter offers betel nuts, coins, rice and chicken and utters his prayers for the blessings of magbabaya. We continue to ask permission from the lesser gods, *tagaliyang* and *tagabito*, so that we may be allowed to enter the cave).

Ocular visits at Rogongon showed that the Higaonon belief on a superbeing is contained in their *gitamod* otherwise known as oral history. Leading baylans like Datu Eladio Sangkuan and Sultan Kaamuran Daranda shared this *"Ang estorya ug kaagi namo nga mga Higaonon maoy gitawag ug gitamod. Ang gitamod mao ang pulong nga nagasikad sa mga gisulti sa ginikanan. Ginakonsiderar namo nga mao kanay kabilin nga among nakuha gikan sa among mga katigulangan. Apan walay nasulat nga makasuporta sa gitamod pero ang amo giila ug gi-observa nga mga pamaagi sa pagrespeto sa kinaiyahan maoy naglig-on sa among pagtuo sa magbabaya. Kaming mga Higaonon sa Rogongon nagahatag ug pagkaon uban sa pag-ampo ngadto sa magbabaya sa usa ka sagrado nga lugar nga mao ang kumba. Ang praktis sa paghalad ug pagkaon nagasukad niadto pang ika-16 siglo. Kadto mao ang bugas, mama, tabako ug ang bisaya nga manok. Ang presensya sa magbabaya mabati kana pinaagi sa sagradong ritwal. Ang magbabaya mohatag ug mensahe o mga laraw kanamo pinaagi sa baylan nganha sa paghalad ug seremonya pinaagi sa pagsulti ug laing pinulungan sa usa ka baylan. Ang paggamit sa bino ug sinsilyo maoy nahimong kaparte sa paghalad ngadto sa magbabaya. Ang among unang mga katigulangan mao ang nakaambit sa paggamit sa kwarta nga nagsimbolo sa puthaw ug ang paggamit sa bino nagsimbolo sa taas nga kinabuhi"* (The oral history and tradition of the Higaonons is called *gitamod*. *Gitamod* includes words which are stated by our parents. We consider these words as legacy from our ancestors. Although no documents could support *gitamod*, we observe practices that concretize our belief on a superbeing. The said belief is manifested in our respect and reverence in nature. We offer food and prayer to our superbeing in a sacred site called *kumba*. The practice of food offering could be traced even earlier than the sixteenth century. It consists of rice, betel nut, tobacco and a native white chicken. The presence of our superbeing could be felt through the sacred ritual. The superbeing sends messages and signs to us during the ceremony through the speaking tongues of the baylans).

Kumba is a site at the interior of the huge forest reserve located at the foothills of Mt. Tambulan. It is the site of ritual offerings among the Higaonon on occasion of thanksgiving in the forest and the asking permission when the hunter intends to venture in the area.

Mc Null Burns (1955) wrote an idea about gods and goddesses in Africa. "The Africans reach and communicate to their gods and goddesses through sacred ritual and magical ceremony. A contact with their deity brings benefits and blessings to their material lives". This is what exactly the Higaonons in Rogongon are doing as confirmed by their datus and baylans. Blair and Robertson (1903) wrote that Spanish colonization in Mindanao influenced the system of currency and use of commodities like wine of the early Filipinos. The Spaniards were able to influence the natives of Mindanao the value of money as means to acquire things and the taste of wine but it has a social and religious functions of the Higaonon as shown in their ritual making. Datu Ayunan shared that the use of wine and coin became a part of their offerings to the superbeing. Their forefathers adopted the use of money to represent a metal and the use of wine for long life. Agoncillo (1990), on his book "History of the Filipino People" stressed that "the ancient Filipinos believed in the ranking deity and a supreme god known as *Bathalang Maykapal*. They respected the host of other deities, in the environmental spirits and in the soul spirits. The early Filipinos adored idols called *anito* in Tagalog and *diwata* in Visayan". The findings of Agoncillo about the environmental spirits and ranking deities are also known among the Higaonons of Rogongon. The Higaonons recognize diwata as good elemental known to them as nature spirits are also the same as those of environmental spirits. These indicates that similar ideas on nature spirits were established during the ancient time. Cole (1956), on his book about the Philippine Islands described fishing as one of the major activities of the early Filipinos. Cole explained that fishing was developed because the settlements of the early Filipinos were mainly situated near the banks of the river system. Datu Mario Daranda shared that *"Ang pagpanguha ug isda alang kanamong mga Higaonon nagasikad gayud sa permiso gikan sa bulalakaw. Kon ang permiso gihatag na uban sa mga espiritu kami dinhi sa Bayog makadawat ug grasya nga abunda sa isda sama sa kasili ug binaw"* (fishing activity among Higaonons requires permission from *Bulalakaw*. With the permission granted by the lesser beings, we collect plenty of fishes in Bayog river. Our catch would vary from *gisaw, kasili* and *binaw*). In an interview with Elidin Lihayan, a hunter, the researcher learned some hunting rituals of the Higaonon. *"Ang pangayam isip usa ka dakong pagpanginabuhi-an naga-agi sa pagpangayo ug katahuran o permiso gikan sa tagabalite ug mga diwata sa lasang. Ang unang katuyu-an niining paghalad mao ang paghatag ug panalangin kanamo gikan sa manlulunda nga maoy nagagiya sa paglatas sa kalasangan alang sa pagpangayam. Ang tagabalite mao ang espiritu sa mga balite ug uban pang kakahuyan ug sa kalasangan nagahatag ug giya ug pagbantay sa kalasangan nagahatag ug giya ug pagbantay sa mangangayam sa pagpangita sa usa"* (Hunting as a major source of livelihood involves a ritual asking permission from *Tagabalite*. The primary purpose of this ritual is to gain approval from the lesser being, who in turn gives permission in crossing the forest for hunting purpose. *Tagabalite*, a lesser god known as the spirit of the trees, grants protection and guides the hunter in his search for wild animals). Joel Timbal, who is also a hunter, pointed out that *"Ang usa ka mangayam nagatudlo nga siya mohatag sa espiritu sa iyang nakuha sa lasang ug mohatag usab siya sa iyang mga kaubanan sa komunidad"* (a hunter should share with the spirits a portion of his catch aside from the share he should set aside for the community as practiced by their ancestors).

Datu Rodulfo So-ong narrated that, *"Ang pagpanguma mao usab pinaka importante nga makakwarta kaming mga Higaonon dinhi sa Rogongon. Ang mag-uuma mohalad sa iyang panalangin sa pagpananghid o ang pagpangayo ug permiso para sa pag-abli sa uma. Ang pagpananghid gihimo aron masiguro ang maayong abut ug ang pagpanalipod sa among uma aron dili anha-un sa mga peste o kalamidad. Ang pagpangayo ug grasya ug sa maayong panlawas. Kauban sa gihalad mao ang usa ka salupan nga humay o mais nga isabud sa kaumahan. Sa panahon sa pag-ani, ang nag-uma maoy mohimo sa lagti. Ang lagti mao ang pagtilaw ug paghalad ug usa ka salupan nga humay lutuon kini ug ihalad ngadto kang magbabaya para sa pagtilaw"* (farming is an important source of income among the Higaonons of Rogongon. The farmer should offer the ritual of asking permission for farm entry. Permission is done to ensure good harvest and protection of our farm against pests and calamities. The blessing for good health is primarily ask from *Apo Nangadun*, the spirit who takes care of good health. Part of the offering includes a handful of grain or corn grits to be showered in the fields. During the harvest season the farmer would perform the *lagti*. *Lagti* refers to the offering of a handful of grains to *magbabaya* for tasting purposes). Moreover Sultan Kaamuran Daranda and a group of bae added *"kami nag-ila kang Apo Pamamahandi a Tolon isip katigulangan nga maoy nagbantay sa among pagpangwarta sama sa abut sa produkto. Ang puthaw mao ang angayan himoon nga gamit para sa panguma. Sa mga tuig ulahi sa ika-19 siglo kami nga mga Higaonons nagasugod sa paggamit ug puthaw para sa pag ugmad sa yuta"* (Apo Pamamahandi a Tolon is the ancestor who takes care of the Higaonon search for wealth which include money as a source of income from their products. Metal is an ideal component for making spears used in farming. In the late nineteenth century the Higaonons started their farming activity with the use of metals).

Datu So-ong further elaborated, *"ang pagpanguma magsugod sa paghilo sa uma nga gitawag ug pangalas. Pangalas mao ang pagputol sa mga kahoy. Ang tabalite mao ang gihalaran niini ug kini mosunod ang pagpangayo ug permiso gikan sa tagabugta ug ibabasuk nga maoy nagbantay sa kayutaan. Ang ritwal maoy makahatag ug maayong abut ug mobantay sa dangan sa uma"* (farming begins with a forest clearing which includes cutting of bushes and trees. The *tagabaite* spirit is directed to this ritual. This is then accompanied with the ritual of asking permission from the *tagabalite* or the *ibabasuk* who guards the farmland. The ritual provides them an assurance of good harvest and assistance to ward off pests in the farm).

Baylan Mangkaliyagan Inloran said, *"Ang manlulunda makadawat ug parehas nga ritwal sa paghalad. Kami nagahimo ug ritwal sa panahon sa pang-uma, pangisda ug pagputol sa kahoy"* (the lesser beings receive equal share in terms of ritual and material offerings. We performed rituals in time of farming, fishing and cutting of trees). Sultan Kaamuran stressed that, *"Ang pagrespeto nagsikad sa manlulunda kay sila ang tuong kamot ni magbabaya. Sila ang gitawag ug manlulunda"* (respect should be addressed to the lesser beings because they serve as the right hand gods known to the Higaonon in Rogongon as *manlulunda*). Moreover, Kagawad Abungan also said that, *"Nagahalad kami ug respeto ug ritwal sa mga manlulunda tungod sa pagbantay nila sa kinabuhi sa mga Higaonon nga mahalikay kami sa kadautan"* (We offer respect and ritual to the lesser beings because they protect us from harm).

One striking similarity among the Chinese and the Higaonons on farming practices is found in their offering to the farmland spirits Kwei and Ibabasuk. The system of farming activity among the Higaonons as attended by the researcher is similar to that of the Chinese which both require an offering of grains in the farmlands and undergo a series of rituals until harvest season (Burns, 1955).

Hopfe (1983) discussed some of the Chinese beliefs in the multiplicity of gods and spirits. He wrote that the earliest religious practice of the Chinese was based upon the recognition of many gods and spirits which control the Universe. He further discussed that Chinese religions had developed a series of rituals that sought to appease the gods and the ancestors. At many point of contact between the Africans and the spirit world, various forms of sacrifices were used to smoothen the way and provide a point of communion between humankind and the spirit world.

The Elementals known as "dili ingon nato"

Demetrio (1990) wrote that *"the engkantos are dili ingon nato or dili parehas.* The *engkanto* dwelt in places which the naked eye can see them as mere boulders, large rocks, mounds on the earth or trees like the balite. The human friends of *engkantos* see them as magnificent palaces and mansions. Their foods is first class but contains no salt.

According to Jose Pandana, *"Ang mga padedeng ug diwata ginarespetuhan usab kana sila namo. Ang mga diwata nga maayo, sila ang mag-abay sa mga baylan aron makagahum kini sa pagkakita ug pagkadungog kanila. Ug gigamhan usab alang sa pag-ayo sa mga masakiton. Kaming mga Higaonon nagatuo usab nga ang mga diwata sa pangpang nga kabatohan, busay sa abaga ug kakahuyan ug mga kantil. Kinahanglan namo nga mangayo ug pananghid ug respeto sa mga diwatas."* (the elementals are also venerated by the Higaonons. Some of the elementals are good. They are known as *diwatas.* They guide a *baylan* and a *datu* who empowered to see the diwatas. A *baylan* may be blessed with the power to cure ailments. The Higaonons believe that these *diwatas* dwell in the rocky cliffs, cascading waters, forested areas and rare places of the valleys. It is necessary for the Higaonons to ask permission and respect the *diwatas.* However, there are also *padedeng.* They inflict harm to anyone else). Mario Daranda shared that *"Kining Padedeng makit-an sa balite. Sila makahatag ug kadautan sama sa buyag. Sila giila nga makabuyag nga moresulta sa sakit sa ulo, pagsuka ug uban pa"* (these elementals are found in the balite trees. They are considered as the cause of illness and other forms of ailments like headache and vomiting).

An incident happened one Tuesday afternoon when a Higaonon cut a branch of an asuete tree without offering a ritual. He suffered from severe headache. In order for the sick person to recover from pain, Baylan Kaamuran performed the ritual of *pagpanawagtawag. Pagpanawagtawag* refers to the calling of attention among the *tagabalite* spirits done at six o'clock in the afternoon. The blood of the chicken was offered at the trunk of the balite. The offering was meant to invoke and ask forgiveness from the *padedeng.* Baylan Kaamuran successfully called the attention of *Nangadun* for healing purposes. Bae Pacita Guicanan commented *"ang padedeng nalipay sa gihimo nga ritwal"* (the Padedeng was delighted when the ritual was performed).

Sultan Bailo Daranda narrated *"Ang ritwal pagahimuon sa oras nga alas singko hangtud sa alas sais. Ang baylan mosulti ug latin nga estorya"* (the rituals are done at dusk between five to six o'clock. The baylan utters words in latin). *"Latin"* refers to a combination of *binukid* and speaking tongue. Speaking tongues are unusual communication of a baylan which consists of several languages uttered simultaneously that may be heard as strange sounds. *Binukid* refers to the dialect used by the Higaonons as a medium of communication while speaking tongue refers to the message of the elementals channeled thru the baylan and spoken by the latter in a language that he alone can understand. The speaking tongues that was uttered by the baylans in Rogongon was an indication that he was possessed by the spirits making him instrumental as healer. The baylan experience of speaking tongues is also similar to the findings of Goodman (1955) among the Maya tribe. He discovered *Glossalia*, *"Glossalia* is a speaking tongue among the Mayas of Latin America. The Mayas utter a sound of different languages when they are possessed by the spirits and channel a message when they are empowered by the speaking tongue".

Datu Bubong Pianza stressed that, *Adunay duha ka klase sa dili ingon nato, ang maayo ug ang dautan. Kana sila nagapuyo sa mga awaaw ug makuyaw nga lugar sama sa pangpang, kabunturan ug kabukiran"* (there are two kinds of elementals namely: the good and the evil. Both dwell in risky places like the cliff, the valleys, the foothills). Datu Rudolfo So-ong revealed that, (*Ang dili ingon nato mopakita pinaagi sa espiritu sa nagkalainlaing hitsura ug sa kadiyut mahanaw lang nga murag panganod. Ang mga padedeng maoy dautan ug mohatag kini ug sakit tungod sa buyag"* (this elementals appear as spirits in multi-dimension. They appear in human personages, animal forms and transform quickly like a silhouette. The *diwatas* provide help and protection to the people. While the *padedeng* cause discomfort). Bae Teresita So-ong explained that, *"mobuyag ang padedeng kon kami makalimot sa paghalad ug pagrespeto kanila"* (when a person trespasses the abode of *padedeng* and failed to offer a ritual of asking permission then discomfort may happen to him).

The Higaonons of Rogongon with the chief baylan Datu Rudolfo So-ong identified *"kami nag-ila sa mga dili ingon nato isip mga padedeng nga dautan ug diwata nga maayo. Kami nagahatag ug pagrespeto ug pangamuyo uban sa sakripisyo aron makuha lang ang ilang kaayo. Ang pag-ampo gihimo usab aron mawala ang ilang kasuko sa tawo"* (these environmental spirits, both the good and bad elementals, whom we offer prayers, rituals and sacrifices to win their goodness. The ritual is also done in order to vanish their anger).

Baylan Daranda Kaamuran, performed ritual in the following manner: He dressed according to the attire of Higaonon tradition. He also wore a red headband symbolizing bravery. He placed a plate of rice, betel nuts, tobacco and wine near the balite tree where the offerings are to be made. He then chants in his own speaking tongue and invokes the bad spirit not to harm the person who will start a farming activity near the balite tree. The offerings and the sacrifices are also done similarly when a person is harmed by the *padedeng*.

Moreover, Datu Mansumayan explained that, *"Ang baylan isip usa ka mananambal nakabaton ug gahum ug adunay mga diwata isip maka-ila ug makasabot niining mga dili ingon nato. Ang baylan usab adunay kahibalo sa mga panambal hilabi na sa yamyam aron mawala ang dautan nga espiritu"* (the baylans take their role as ritualist and healers because they possess extra powers and they have abyan spirit to guide them in identifying and understanding the forces of nature. A baylan also possess knowledge in herbal medicines and in saying used to ward off bad spirits).

The Mangyan belief in the elementals were described as follows: "the invisible spirits are the different kinds—the good and the bad. The person whom the good spirits take possession of, implore the bad spirits not to harm them. The spirits prohibit them from destroying the environment. They will be punished if they do so. If the sick Mangyan do not get well, it means that they have desecrated the places of the anitos. They first speak with the spirits as to what ritual is to be done. The *shamans* act like doctors who speak to the spirits." The *Shamans* among the Mangyans are those persons engaged in ritual making and healing with the use of herbal medicines (Mercado, 1999).

Spirits of Dead Ancestors

The researcher's informants, Datu Ayunan and Carlito So-ong, shared that *"nagahatag kami ug dakong respeto o bili sa kalag ug mga espiritu sa among nangamatay nga katigulangan"* (we set priorities and give high regard to the spirits of our dead ancestors). Cabiladas (1999) wrote an article entitled *The Sacred History of the Kingdom of Tagolo-an* mentioned that, *"Apo Sominam-ang kon Tominokol usa ka unang mangingisda. Si Apo adunay usa ka pamalandong ug ang usa ka diwata mikunsad kaniya ug nagatudlo kaniya ngadto sa tinubdan sa bayog nga suba ug kini giila sa ngalan nga busay Limunsudan. Ug kini naga-ingon nga ang anghel nagsulti kaniya sa pagsubay sa suba sa bayog, siya ug ang iyang katawhan naluwas sa dakong lunop. Kami nga mga Higaonon naga-ingon nga ang sumusunod ni Apo Sominam-ang nagahigugma kaniya tungod sa iyang maayong binuhatan, kaming mga Higaonon naga-ingon nga siya luwas na ni magbabaya. Si Apo Sominam-ang uban sa iyang katigulangan gisulod namo sa among huna-huna. Ang mga datu naga-ingon nga ang mga katigulangan apil sa ilang pag-ampo".* (Apo *Sominam-ang kon Tominokol* was the first settler of Bayog who lived as a fisherman. Apo *Sominam-ang* once had a meditation and a fairy appeared mandating him to trace the source of Bayog river of what is now the *Limunsudan Falls.* The account further stated that, the fairy told him that by tracing the source of Bayog river, he and his people will be saved from the great flood. The Higaonons added that the descendants of Apo Sominam-ang highly revered him because of his good deeds. They named him as *Lingas* meaning saved by magbabaya. Apo Sominam-ang together with the ancestors were treasured in the memory of the Higaonons in Rogongon. The datus claim that their ancestors are part of their rituals). Aside from the story of Apo Sominam-ang, Cabiladas (1999) added that the sacred history includes the story of the following ancestors namely: *Apo Migsuanob, Apo Imbalagil, Apo Makaupaw, Apo Balingbingan, Apo Palatambol su Palakampana, Apo Banlag, Apo Agyo, Apo Amantaw-antaw, Apo Dalinasan, Apo Pamulaw and Apo Magbabasuk.* Datu Bubong observed that the stories of these ancestors were orally taught by the Higaonon parents and treasured in their memory known as *gitamod.* Hence, *gitamod* served as an oral historical account.

Datu Eladio Sangkuan stressed that, *"nagatahud kami sa among katigulangan kay sila man ang nakasunod sa maayong sugo ug pamatasan. Ang espiritu sa among katigulangan maoy nagbantay kanamo aron sa among kalihukan ug panginabuhian. Ang among panginabuhian gigiyahan sa magbabaya, ang magbabasuk ug ang mga katigulangan"* (we respect our ancestors who heartily follow the god's mandate. The spirits of our ancestors protect us in our activities and sustainance. We are guided by the magbabaya, by the magbabasuk and by our ancestors).

He further recounted that, *"Si Apo Palakampana ang nahabilin sa lunop. Naluwas siya pinaagi sa paglakaw gikan sa dagat ngadto sa bukid. Si Palakampana nakaabot sa tumoy sa bukid Tambulan. Usa ka butang nga siya naluwas tungod sa iyang paglakaw nagatambul usab siya sa iyang kawayan nga dala aron moundang ang lunop. Sa laing bahin, Si Apo Pamulaw nagahimo ug sakripisyo aron maluwas sa pulaw o kainit. Miadto siya sa kalatungan nga bukid ug naga-ampo sa magbabaya ug sa ibunturon sa ilang kalooy. Si Apo Pamulaw naluwas pinaagi sa pag-usap ug mama sa sulod sa kapulaw o sa unom ka bulan nga panahon sa kainit, didto sa estorya ni Pamulaw nga ang mama nahimong importante sa paghalad"* (Apo *Palakampana* was one of the survivors of the flood. He saved himself by walking from the seacoast to the foot of the mountain. *Apo Palakampana* reached the peak of Mt. Tambulan. He was saved by beating his bamboo pole while he walked, and this stopped the flood. On the other hand, *Apo Pamulaw* made a sacrifice to stop the months of long drought. He went to Mt. Kalatungan and prayed to the Magbabaya and to the lesser beings for mercy. Apo Pamulaw survived by chewing betel nuts throughout the long drought. It was the story of Apo Pamulaw which made the betel nuts a significant component of ritual).

Mercado (1998), wrote in his findings about the Mangyans that "when a person dies, he returns to the environment and becomes dust. Man therefore should respect the environment because it is where their ancestors lived. The environment, therefore, is sacred". This is also true to the Higaonons, they respect their environment to pay respect to their ancestors.

The book of Agoncillo (1990) included a belief in life after death. There is a relationship between the dead and the living as observed by the early Filipinos. A sign of respect to their dead is also being observed by the Higaonons of Rogongon. They give reverence to their dead ancestors, a practice which had been handed to them from their forefathers.

Inanimate Objects known as *"Bala-ang Butang"*

Gloria (1989) discussed the importance of inanimate objects as a living treasure inherited from their parents. She further explained that objects even of a little kind is important especially if that is inherited from their parents. The material things such as depository box, kris, laddle and weighing scale are among the sacred objects valued by the Higaonons as a sign of respect to their ancestors. The Higaonon baylans and datus in Rogongon have a common belief in weighing scale known to them as *"gantangan o tagulambong pandaut sulutan"*. A weighing scale symbolizes the Higaonon's justice system. This is used when an oath of truth is made until peace is achieved. The weighing scale of the Higaonons is made up of a round and concave, circular piece of wood. It can contain eight glasses of rice which is equivalent to one and a half kilo. *tagulambong pandaut sulutan* is known for its accuracy. In fact the Council of Baylans, Datus and elected Peace Council of the Higaonon use it during decision-making. *Tagulambong Pandaut Sulutan* has been proven effective in feuds, conflicts and resolutions. Datu Rodulfo So-ong narrated that, *"Bisan unsay among kalapasan sama sa kostumbre masulbad kini pinaagi sa timbangan pandaut sulutan. Si Diwata Kahungko sa Lasang maoy nanag-iya niini"* (any violation of Higaonon customary law are resolved using the weighing scale. *Diwata Kahungko sa Lasang* is the owner of this thing). Cabiladas (1999), in his article, *The Sacred History of the Higaonon,* mention that, *"Ang timbangan maoy gamiton sa pagsulbad sa problema. Ang pagsulbad sa problema sa mga kayugot pagahimuon sa tampuda ho balagon, ang itlog pagabu-akon ug ang oway putlon. Kini nga buhat nagaputol usab sa kayugot nga nag timaan sa itlog ug oway"* (the weighing scale is used in settling conflicts. To resolve the conflict an oath is done in the green vine branch also known as peace pact. To be able to take an oath for justice towards peace, an egg has to be broken and a piece of rattan has to be cut. This act signifies the breaking of feud and cutting of conflict as symbolized by the egg and rattan). This ceremony is being attended by the datus and the baylans who attest its making. The individuals involved in the feud have to take an oath with the conviction that the spirits are watching them all throughout the ceremony. The Higaonon baylans said that, *"Ang manlulunda o diwata nga nagsaplid mao si Ananaplid. Si Diwata Ananampok maoy nagbantay sa oway ug si Diwata Amomogpog maoy sa itlog".* (the lesser beings who take charge of the accuracy of the measurement is Diwata Ananaplid. Diwata Ananampoc takes charge of the rattan while Diwata Amomogpog takes charge of the egg).

Higaonon antiques are considered precious legacies and they can be inherited. Datu Eladio shared a story, *"Ang bangkaw maoy gamiton sa pagdakop sa mga usa ug baboy sulop. Ang mangayam nagamit ug pahawan isip proteksyon sa pagpangayam. Salikot maoy pisi gamiton aron paghikot sa baboy sulop"* (a spear is used in hunting the wild animals. The hunter uses shield for protection while hunting. *Salikot* refers to a rope used in tying a captured wild pig and *kalasag* refers to a horn of a deer or carabao are kept as a legacy of the early hunters). Other sacred inanimate objects of the Higaonons according to Carlito So-ong includes the following, *"Ang yahong usa ka antic nga balaang butang nga gamiton para sudlanan sa mama. Ang tilad nagalangkob sa tabako ug humay".* (a bowl, which is both antique and sacred is used as container for the *tilad* consisted of betel nuts, tobacco and rice). He also share that, *"ang yuta usab usa ka kabilin sa among ginikanan ug tuburan sa panginabuhi"* (a piece of land, which is an ancestral domain, is also an important source of livelihood). Onos Daranda added that *kaban* (box), *tibud* (small box), *sundang* (sharp-bladed bolo), kris *(kasilayan),* nose rope *(tango),* and other material possession left from their forefathers are also considered sacred. Vestiges of the Higaonon possession of these materials were owned by the baylans and the datus. The weighing scale symbolizes truth and accuracy, weapons symbolizes bravery while precious things such as jewelry box reflect their social status because of its historical value.

CHAPTER 3

Myth, Epic and Legend

Table below shows the Myth, Epic and Legend of the Higaonon Tribal Identity

Myth	Beliefs
Apo Sominam-ang	The first Higaonon ancestor who traveled from the source of Bayog towards *pultahan sa langit* by foot and empowered by the diwata sa *lingas*
Apo Dalinason	The first baylan who reached *pultahan sa langit* and empowered as the great healer
Apo Agyo	The great tribal leader of Tagoloan, Cagayan, Bayog and Butuan who reached *pultahan sa langit*
Epic	**Beliefs**
Sala	Song of courtship and love chanted on marriage festivity
Darinday	Song for acquaintances chanted during merrymaking
Ulaging	Chanted during the Kaamulan festivity
Legend	**Beliefs**
Limunsudan Falls	*Pultahan sa langit* or entrance to heaven; home of the *manlulunda* (right hand of the *magbabaya*); meeting place of the spirits or *diwatas* which empowered blessings towards dead ancestors
Bayog River	The way towards *pultahan sa langit* early ancestors walked in that river like walking in a pavement
Rogongon	Came from a word *logong* means a place of thunder due to the huge thunder like sounds as trees presses its branches; magbabaya called the spirits to meet in that place

Sturtevant as quoted by Gloria (1987), wrote that "myths include stories that narrate the basic values and absolute truths about the cultural practices of man. These values had been transcended from generation to generation". Gloria added that, "the origins and beginnings of non-literate people are preserved in their oral tradition especially in their myths and legends". The myths and legends of the Higaonons are expressed in the form of songs and stories shared by their ancestors to them through oral tradition.

Cabiladas (1999) wrote about the Higaonons in Rogongon *"Ang Higaonon nagapuyo sa ilang tinuohang istorya ika-14 siglo. Usa sa ilang pagtuo mao si Apo Sominam-ang kon Tominokol, ang pinakabantog nga tigulang"* (the Higaonons have a story which can be traced back during the fourteenth century. One of their story is about *Apo Sominam-ang kon Tominokol*, the great Higaonon ancestor). Datu Sandigan sa Bayog further wrote an article in 1998 that, *"Sa wala pa ang Muslim niadtong ika-14 siglo ang Higaonon sa Rogongon nakahigayon sa pakigbaligya sa ilang produkto pinaagi sa pakig-baylo. Ang mga Intsik mianhi sa Pilipinas sa panahon adtong Tang Dynasty sa Tsina. Sila nagapabaylo sa among produkto ug kami nagpuyo sa daplin sa dagkong suba, sama sa Butuan, Tagoloan, Cagayan ug Bayog. Ang datu sa Rogongon nag-ingon nga si Apo Sominam-ang gikunsaran sa ispiritu sa kaluwasan didto sa Limunsudan."* (before the coming of the Muslim Arab Missionaries in the fourteenth century, the Higaonons in Rogongon had already established a trading contact through barter (Datu Sandigan sa Bayog, 1999). The Chinese traders came to the Philippines during the Tang Dynasty of China. They traded with the Higaonons who settled in the river banks of the big river system of Butuan, Tagoloan, Cagayan and Bayog. The Datus in Rogongon believed that Apo Sominam-ang kon Tominokol was blessed by the spirits of the Limunsudan falls).

The Higaonons of Rogongon shared a story about Apo Dalinason. *"Si Apo Dalinason maoy pinaka-una nga baylan sa Rogongon ug gitoohan nga gikunsaran sa diwata tungod sa iyang kanunay nga pag-ampo ngadto sa Magbabaya. Misaka sa langit ug nagsubay sa tinugdan sa suba nga Bayog nga maoy gitawag nga pultahan sa langit, kami nga mga Higaonon dinhi sa Rogongon nagtamod kaniya isip usa ka luwas"* (Apo Dalinason was the first baylan in Rogongon and believed to have been empowered by the diwata because of his constant rituals to the magbabaya. He ascended to heaven following the source of Bayog river system which they believe as an entrance to heaven. The descendant of Apo Dalinason called him *lingas*, meaning once saved from sins). This story is admired by the descendants because of Apo Dalinason's strong faith to magbabaya. The source of Bayog river system known as Limunsudan Falls is considered a sacred place because it was where the soul of Apo Dalinason was blessed by the magbabaya. The Higaonons in Rogongon gave high reverence to Apo Sominam-ang and Apo Dalinason whom they considered as immortals.

Kaamulan festival is being observed by the Higaonons as the traditional way of tracing orally the history of their ancestors. They hold the said festival once a year. During this time, the baylans and datus in Rogongon relate the great stories to the community. They cleverly trace genealogies and significant stories during the festival. Prominent were those of the lineage of Apo Sominam-ang and among others. The main aim of the festival is to sustain the knowledge of the Higaonons concerning their tribal identity.

Sala is a Higaonon epic which involves singing during courtship. The father of the suitor will render a song. It is through singing that the suitor is able to express his love for the lady. The parents of the lady give their consent and schedule of wedding. *Sala* is always the basis of the Higaonon social condition which serve as the basis of their tribal identity.

Unabia (1996), wrote the following example of *sala* which was also observed by the Higaonons of Rogongon, Quoted herein is a sala which reflects the idea of beauty, love and acceptance of the proposed marriage.

"Sala Hu Agkabisitahan ha Laga, Buyawan ka Indasun ha din-ayun sa napuunan, Gimba sa indagandan Ha yawed sa nagikanan, Inbeleng ka mangena Na mindan ka mangalendem, Ta hadi ha makagmama. Na hadi ka makgyapunhan"

Darinday is an epic that is used for many occasions. It is during acquaintances and matrimonial festivities. *Darinday* varies in tune and lyrics depending whether it is for acquaintance or matrimonial ceremony. An example of *Darinday* as chanted by Datu Eladio Sangkuan is as follows:

"Yamba tagsa, yamba tagsum; Gaya ina, singgilanta Dinayunta, aagani; Disuanay, Pamulawi, Pamulawo. Inayan tupaganay; Diyanapa, tagna-iya Duway talaya, nangadansa".

The epic according to Datu Eladio Sangkuan refers to the idea of happiness, hope blessings and good health. This is translated in the Visayan translation which goes like this *"Mauba siya, siya ba gayud ang nagpakita sa krosing sa dalan nga akong gi-alimahan, nga akong gi-ampingan, maanyag nga dalaga, gwapa nga babaye, anakan sa una, anak sa una duhay asawa apan siya ang akong gihigugma".*

The legends of the Higaonon in Rogongon is inscribed in their memory. The oral account of the informants was narrated by the datus and baylans. A remarkable story of the Higaonon origin was entertwined with that of the existence of the Bayog river and its source the *Abaga sa Bayog* known as *Limunsudan Falls*. *Limunsudan Falls*, bestowed to be the gateway to heaven, is located in a deep ravine twenty-eight kilometers from Rogongon proper and could be reached by walking for almost nine (9) hours. The falls is heavily surrounded by tropical forest. Baylan Mang Katodo related an oral account that *"Ang lugar maoy puloy-anan sa ibunturon ug ispiritu diin ang Magbabaya mohatag ug gahom pinaagi sa Manlulunda nga anaa sa busay Limunsudan"* (the place is the home of the lesser gods and spirits wherein the magbabaya extends his power through his *manlulunda* known as the lesser gods in this *Limunsudan Falls*). Mang Singyan also related that *"kana nga lugar usa ka balaan tungod kay mao kana ang puy-anan ni Magbabaya ug Manlulunda. Kami nga mga Higaonon nagatoo nga ang lugar maoy pultahan sa langit"* (the place is sacred because that is the dwelling place of a superbeing and the lesser beings. The Higaonons of Rogongon believed that the place is the gateway to heaven). Inay Garingay Salana said that *"Ang langit maabot pinaagi niining ganghaan"* (heaven could be reached through this entrance). Mang Cunto narrated that *"Ang sinugdanan namong mga Higaonon sa Rogongon mataga-ag bili ngadto kang Agyo, isip usa ka lider sa tribo sa Tagoloan, Butuan ug Bayog".*(the origin of the Higaonon ancestors of Rogongon is accounted to *Apo Agyo* who was the tribal leader of the Tagoloan, Butuan and Bayog). Mang Paser Sayana narrated that *"Si Agyo adunay panaw gikan sa baybay ug siya gibayog uban sa iyang bangka ngadto sa ganghaan sa suba sa Bayog paingon sa abaga niini"* (Agyo cruise from the seacoast. In the event of his journey, a huge wind blew his boat and carried him to Bayog river towards the entrance of Limunsudan Falls).

The study of Tuante (1998), entitled *The History of Bayug* cited the origin of the name Bayog and is accounted to the term *gibayog* meaning blown by the wind referring to a tribal chieftain who was blown by the wind on the course of his journey. Castro (1998) also mentioned that Agyo has a wider extent of influence and leadership in as far as Northern Mindanao.

In an interview with Mang Bulanay Salana, he narrated that *"Ang sinugdan namong mga Higaonon ug kang Apo Agyo maoy makahimo ug pinuy-anan dinhi sa Rogongon. Ang lugar nga nag-ingon sa sinultihan nga logong o tingog sa dalogdog niadtong panahon sa lunop"* (the origin of the Higaonons to that of Apo Agyo has relatively develop a settlement of Rogongon, a term originally known as logong meaning a huge thunder that struck during the great flood). Mang Salana elaborated that *"Ang dalogdog nga nadungog ni Agyo adtong panahon sa lunop sa maong pagbiyahe nakagiya kaniya sa tinugdan sa abaga"* (the thunder that was heard by the

Agyo during the flood on his journey to Bayog led him to the source of the falls). Moreover, Datu Bubong Pianza narrated that the great flood long time ago which brought Apo Agyo in the traces of Bayog river going through Limunsudan falls develop a settlement among his later generation. Oral history on the other hand provides that the place has been the origin of the huge sounds that could be heard like thunder. According to informants that the thunder-like sounds are those trees which presses its branches then produce sounds. The sounds believed by the early ancestors as the call of *magbabaya* to settle in the area as shared by informants. In the article of Cabiladas written in 1999 proved that the presence of Bayog river provided access among the trading contacts of the Higaonon and the Chinese traders during the Tang dynasty. Informants said that the migrations of people in the hinterlands in the sixteenth century and as supported by the work of Tuante (1998) about the migrations of people from the coast towards the hinterland develop a settlement in Rogongon.

CHAPTER 4

The Higaonon Landmarks and Sacred Sites

The table below shows the Higaonon landmarks and sacred sites

Landmarks/ sacred sites	Location from Rogongon proper	Beliefs
A. Mountain Mt. Tambulan	15 km Northeast	Home of Apo Palatambul who was saved from the great flood
Mt. Ligui	10 km South	Place of Apo Mangawan's hideout
Mt. Dungguan	17 km East	Home of diwata Pinag-aso
Mt. Kalatungan	13 km Southwest	Apo Pamulaw and Apo Insayan saved from drought
Mt. Tominukas	13 km Southerst	Apo Tominukas achieved his immortality
Mt. Pilo-asan	13 km Southwest	Home of Apo Pinighawan where he received his salvation
B. Gravesites	0.5 km Northeast	Home of the dead ancestors magbabaya radiated his power
C. Kumba	14 km Northeast at the foothills of Mt. Tambulan	Traditional ritual sites meeting place of the lesser gods where magbabaya extended his power
D. Sagyaan Cave	15 km North	Home of Tagabito and Tagaliyang
E. Baka Baka	18 km South	Home of *tagabato*
F. Limunsudan Falls	17 km Southeast	Dwelling place of manlulunda and home of the bulalakaw and tagabusay

Section 23 of the Republic Act 8371 states: "the Indigenous People's right to religious, cultural ceremonies and sites. The act further provides Indigeous people have the 1.) The right to manifest, practice, develop and teach their spiritual and religious traditions, customs and ceremonies 2.) the right to maintain, protect and have access to their religious and cultural sites 3.) the right to use and control of ceremonial objects 4.) the right to repatriation of human remains. The state take effective measures, in cooperation with the Indigenous people concerned to ensure that Indigenous sacred places including burial sites, be preserved, respected and protected".

Generally, the Higaonon ancestors on account of their oral history provided myth and identified sites that are the abode of the spirits. It is where the ancestors revealed spiritual powers, immortality and salvation from sins. Those landmarks according to Datu Gunzi were verbally transferred and given to them by the their ancestors. According to him *"kanang yutang timailhan maoy buhing handumanan ug laraw sa mga sumusunod nga ang Magbabaya nagaluwas kanamo kon adunay maayong binuhatan"* (these landmarks trace a living example, a turning point, and a reflection to the Higaonon descendants that magbabaya saves people with righteous deeds). The Higaonon showed their reverence and faith by saying a prayer directly to the *magbabaya,* performing rituals, offering food and *tilad* consisting the betel nut, tobacco and buyo leaves being offered to each respective places as landmark of heritage.

Kagawad Paulino Guicanan shared that, *"Kami nga mga Higaonon sa Rogongon nagarespeto sa mga yutang timailhan, isip lugar nga nabantog tungod kay pinuy-anan sa mga espiritu sukad sukad".* (We, the Higaonons in Rogongon, revere these landmarks and sites since time immemorial). Their spiritual belief coupled with myths develop the reverence they manifest in these landmarks and sites which include the mountain, gravesites, rivers, rocks and caves. The Higaonons of Rogongon respect these landmarks because according to Datu Luciano, *"Ang lugar maoy labing dakong istorya nga buot mailhan sumala sa tinuohan ug sa presensya sa espiritu nga naglantaw sa kinabuhi"* (the place is referred to as worthy of historical recognition by the Higaonon's belief on the existence of spirits who oversee their lives). The City Planning on Rogongon Agro Forestry recognized these sites in 1995.

The Higaonons of Rogongon consider the following mountains as sacred sites:

Mt. Tambulan is the highest mountain in Rogongon located fifteen kilometers northeast of barangay Rogongon proper. The Higaonon also named it as *Mt. Gabunan* because it is heavily covered with fog. It also earned the name *Mt. Tambulan* out of the story of *Apo Palatambul su Palakampana*. It was in this mountain where *Apo Palatambul* kept on beating his bamboo pole as he called for help from the lesser being of that mountain. Datu Kaamuran said that *"Si Apo Palatambul naluwas sa lunop wala man miabot sa tumoy sa bukid. Ug kana gitoohan nga ang iyang kaluwasan tungod man sa pagbantay sa diwata"* (Apo Palatambul was saved because the floodwater never rose to the mountain peak. It was believed that *Apo Palatambul's* survival was accounted to the presence of the diwatas who saved *Apo Palatambul* on that event). According to the baylans, *"Ang paagi sa pagrespeto niining lugar nga timailhan mao ang paghalad ug pag-ampo nga sukad sa katigulangan maoy gitawag ug pista sa lasang nga nailhan usab nga panalikot. Sa maong higayon, kaming mga Higaonon nagahalad sumala sa naandan nga puti nga manok, tabako ug mama".* (the way to respect this landmark is manifested in our offerings and that ritual especially during *Pista sa Lasang*. In this occasion we hold thanksgiving to the lesser beings and to our ancestors *Apo Palatambul* who survive by offering the traditional native white chicken, tobacco and betel nuts). Recent offerings of the Higaonon tribal ritual is performed in the Higaonon social hall setting known as *talapnay* instead of performing it in the traditional *kumba*. The *talapnay* is set in a decorated wall with a five meter white cloth hang over the wall within the social hall building. The white cloth is set with decoration of betel nut leaves and young coconut leaves which signify nature in behalf of the traditional *kumba*. In addition with the leaves set therein, a plate with betel nuts, tobacco, rice and coin are offered generally for the occasion of thanksgiving.

Mt. Ligui is another sacred landmark which is located ten kilometers south from Rogongon proper. Datu Passer Lihayan narrated that, *"kining bukira maoy tago-anan sa among katigulangan labi na si Apo Mangawan gikan sa iyang mga kaaway. Kaming mga sumusunod ni Apo Mangawan moagi sab nianang bukira tungod sa pag-agni sa mga Kristiyanos"* (this mountain used to be the hideout of our ancestors under the leadership of Apo Mangawan against his tribal enemy. The descendants of Apo Mangawan retreated in this mountain against the inroads of Christian preachers in the sixteenth century). In an interview with Bologtohan Salahay, he related that, *"Ang bukid Ligi maoy lugar diin si Apo Mangawan gikunsaran sa espiritu ug siya naluwas"* (Mt. Ligi is a place where Apo Mangawan was blessed by the lesser spirits).

Mt. Dungguan is located seventeen kilometers from the East Rogongon proper. It is a significant site considered by the Higaonons. Bologtohan Salahay shared that *"Ang tanang klase sa hayopan nasalbar niining dakong lunop sa maong bukid tungod kay wala misaka ang tubig sa taas nga dapit. Nanganlan ug dungguan ang lugar tungod sa pagdunggo sa mga hayop didto sa tungod kay gibantayan sa mga espiritu. Si Apo Mangawan naluwas usab sa kasal-anan tungod sa espiritu sa bukid sa Dungguan"* (All kinds of animal species in Rogongon were saved from the great flood because the water never rose at the peak of that mountain. *Mt. Dungguan* earned the name *Dunggo* meaning dock because it is the mountain where the animals docked and so they were saved and protected by the spirits from drowning. Apo Mangawan was immortalized and saved by the spirits in *Mt. Dungguan*).

Another sacred mountain considered by the Higaonons according to the key informants is thirteen kilometers southwest of Rogongon proper. These adjacent mountains ranges includes *Mt. Kalatungan* where *Apo Pamulaw* and *Apo Insayun* were blessed by the spirits, *Mt. Tuminukas* is also recognized by the Higaonon ancestors because it is where *Apo Tuminukas* received his salvation and became immortal. *Mt. Piloasan* is sacred because it is where *Apo Pinighawan* was made immortal by the lesser spirits.

Gravesites are sacred places and are located near their homestead such as in the backyards of the Higaonon territory prior to the introduction of public cemetery in the sixteenth century. Alvin Cunto shared an old practice of preserving their dead during the tenth to fifteenth century. According to Alvin Cunto *"Ang patay nga lawas isulod sa kahoy ug biyaan hangtod sa tulo ka bulan didto sa iyahang balay. Human sa ikatulo ka bulan, ang paryente mobisita ngadto ug tan-awon ang patay nga lawas, kon nalata dili siya luwas sa iyang kasal-anan. Kon mawala ang patay nga lawas ug ang beste lang ang mabilin, nagpasabot nga siya luwas".* (the dead is placed in a carved wood leaving it for three months within the home of the concerned family. After one month the relative visit the home where the dead was placed and if only the cloth of the dead is found therein sinifies immortality and they believed that the body and spirits ascended to heaven. But if the corpse decayed this signifies mortality).

Kumba is a traditional ritual sites within the foothills and forested sites of *Mt. Tambulan*. The *kumba* of the Higaonon is equivalent to the Cathedral of the Christian. It is a place where the baylans offer their prayers. *Kumba* is sacred among the Higaonons of Rogongon because it is where the *Panalikot* or *Pista sa Lasang* is held. A *Pista sa Lasang* is a yearly gathering of baylans who performed the *kadilayan*. *Kadilayan* is a ritual of thanksgiving offered to *magbabaya,* to the lesser beings' and to the Higaonon's dead ancestors.

Sagyaan Cave is a sacred place. It is located fifteen kilometers north from the Poblacion of Rogongon. Oral accounts of Inay Tingol Cunto revealed that, *"Ang among katigulangan naghalad ngadto kang Magbabaya nianang lugara nga gitawag nga langob sa Sagyaan".* (our forefathers used to offer rituals to magbabaya in that place). She further recounted *"mao pud na ang lugar diin tago-anan kanamo dinhi sa panahon sa Hapon".* (it also served as the hideout of our ancestors during the Japanese occupation). The cave, as estimated by the informants, can accommodate one to two hundred natives at the same time.

Baka Baka is the biggest rock located in Panonoroganan also known as the Old Rogongon eighteen kilometers from the Rogongon proper. The oral tradition as recounted by the datus, *"gituohan nga nagbantay kanamo nga mangangawan gikan sa mabangis nga sulop".* (believed to be the protector of the Higaonon hunters from harm against wild beast). The Higaonon hunters believe that if the ritual is performed, the spirit of the rocks known as *tagabato* will protect and guide the hunters for his safety.

Limunsudan Falls and **Bayog River** are both legendary and mythical. The falls is located twenty-seven kilometers southeast of Rogongon. The river system started from the basin of the falls transcending through the coast of barangay Bayug in Iligan City. The oral tradition provides that, *"ang Manlulunda sa Magbabaya nagapuyo nianang abaga"* (the right hand of the magbabaya dwells in that falls). Cabiladas (1999), on the *Sacred History of Bayog* mentioned that *"Si Apo Sominam-ang nga maoy sinugdan sa among katigulangan giluwas sa espiritu tungod sa iyang kaayo nganha sa abaga sa Limunsudan"* (Apo Sominam-ang kon Tominokol was blessed by the spirits and believed to be the tribal origin of the Higaonon ancestors).

All these sites were identified by the Higaonons in Rogongon as sacred since time immemorial and are still recognized by them until present. The introduction of Spanish policy known as Reduccion policy (1781) which aimed at the layouting of public plazas, public halls, cemeteries, and recreation center were those new development in the area. The development were recognized by them while continuing their respect on their traditional sites. Moreover, the creation of the Department of Mindanao and Sulu as a decentralized administration of the Americans in Mindanao from 1903 to 1920 (Gowing, 1987) created the policy of attraction such as the construction of roads, public buildings like barangay halls and schools in Rogongon starting 1970. These changes were accepted by the Higaonons with a condition that their sacred sites and landmarks must be observed by the visitors, researchers and businessmen who came to the area. In this regard, the Policy makers through the National Commission on Indigenous People must duly implement and coordinate the Higaonon regarding the existing laws for their benefit and further identify these sacred sites and landmarks.

CHAPTER 5

The Social Impact from Migrants

Higaonon Social Conditions

Social Conditions	Perceptual Beliefs
Social System	Family is the basic unit of the Higaonon society; Male occupied the highest strata; Male title include datu, baylan and Sultan; Bae ranks second in the Higaonon social stratification; Marriage is pre-arranged by parents
Kinship Pattern	Patriarchal descent; Male as the head of the family, disciplinarian and the provider; Polygamy or plural marriages are practiced and accepted; Procreation is sacred
Value System	Observance of customary law, morality, obedience, respect, sharing and honesty
Material Culture and World View	House architectural designs symbolize simplicity and openness; later it has walls for protection purposes; gantangan is used as a symbol for justice and peace; the living and the world of spirits were entertwined

Social System

Smith as quoted by Layton (1997), stressed that "social system proposed an interaction theory. According to this theory that the social order emerges from the interaction of individuals pursuing their self interest". Mama Komunog shared that *"Ang pamilya mao ang pinakagamay nga sumbanan namo. Ug ang lalaki mao ang pinakataas nga hut-ong sa komunidad"* (the family is the basic unit of the Higaonon family and the male occupies the highest strata in the Higaonon community). Sultan sa Limunsudan also shared *"mao kini ang titulo sa mga lalaki: ang datu, ang sultan ug ang baylan. Mao kini ang naandan nga hut-ong hangtud karon. Ilang gipataas ang impluwensya dinha sa komunidad. Ug kining titulo isip usa ka sultan, baylan o datu gipili kini gikan sa ilang katigulangan nga maoy naghatag ug responsibilidad. Bisan sa bag-ong sistema, ang naandan gihapon ang nagpatigbabaw"* (the following are the male title: a datu, a sultan, a baylan. These are the traditional social hierarchy of the Higaonons in Rogongon and even until today. They had extended their influence to the community. The traditional leadership of a datu, a sultan and a baylan is chosen from a forefather whom the one bestowed the responsibility. Even with the advent of political leadership, this traditional system continued and still functional).

Sultan sa Limunsudan also shared that *"Ang baylan, sultan, ug datu maoy mga titulo sa komunidad nga naandan. Ilang gipadako ang ilang katungod isip lider kung gikinahanglan. Ang baylan dunay duha ka klase: bayan sa ritwal, ug ang baylan sa kaligaon. Ang baylan sa kaligaun mao ang mag-una sa pagbuhat sa iyang katungod sa kaliga o ang pagbatbat sa istorya. Adunay linya sa mga sultan: ang kabugatan, radiamuda, padaadin ug ang imam. Ang Sultan sa Limunsudan nag-ingon nga ang iyang gahom magalangkob ug pipila sa iyang katigulangan sa ato pa sinunod. Sa dugang usab ang naandan nga balaud sa Higaonon nag-ingon nga ang baylan ug ang datu maoy tawo nga parehas ang husga nga maoy makasulbad sa problema, makahapsay sa kalinaw, ug ang ritwal. Siya usab makabuhat sa pagminyo, bunyag, ug lubong nga seremonyas. Ang bae maoy tuong kamot sa iyang bana isip sultan ug tabangan niya ang pagbantay sa kahusay ug kalinaw alang sa kabayn-an"* (the Baylan, Sultan and the Datu are the traditional social hierarchy of the Higaonon. They extend their influence to the community if deemed qualified of being a traditional chief. The Baylan which has of two kinds" the *Baylan sa Ritwal* and the *Baylan sa Kaliga-on*. The *Baylan sa ritwal* is the one who led the prayer and the ritual on any traditional occasion. While the *Baylan sa Kaliga-on* will performed his duty as a sole chief on the occasion of *Kaliga* wherein the storytelling of history is performed. The Sultan has a line of assistants consisting of the *Kabugatan*, the *radiamuda*, the *padaadin* and the *imam*. As a Sultan sa Limunsudan, he stated that their power is extended and chosen by their ancestor and is therefore hereditary. Moreover customary law of the Higaonon specifies that a *baylan* or a *datu* is a man of fair judgement who can resolve conflict, maintain peace, perform healing and rituals. He can officiate marriage rites, baptism and burial ceremony. Another honorary leader of the Higaonon community is the *bae*. She functions as the right hand of her husband. The following roles are: maintain peace, a secretary, and act as an adviser to the female residents). Datu Onos Daranda shared that *"Ang naandan nga pagminyo gihimo kini sa mga ginikanan nga gitawag ug pamuya. Kung mo-edad na ug ika-18 ang lalaki ug ika-15 anyos ang babaye kana mahimo na sa istorya sa duha ka ginikanan. Ang paghatag sa lugbak nga naglangkob sa puting panapton ug dagom nga ihatod sa balay sa babaye aron pagsita sa kasabutan. Ang sala mao usab ang pagtan-aw sa kina-iya sa pamilya sa babaye. Mao pud ang insaktong panahon sa ginikanan sa babaye nga ang tumang tuyo nianang panahon. Ang ginikanan sa babaye mohatag usab sa tubag. Unang tubag dili gusto, iuli kini ang lugbak. Ang obligasyon sa paghatag ug lilay nag-adto sa taga-bayn-an maoy gitawag nga 'batang sa bansa' ang naandan nga lilay mao ang yuta niadtong ika-16 nga sigo. Ang puthaw ug kwarta giila kana sa karong kabagho-an".* (the traditional marriage syatem of the Higaonon is pre-arranged by both parents known as *pamuya*. When a boy reaches the age of eighteen and the girl fifteen then that is already the start of a proper negotiation between the boy and his father. The first step is evident by giving a *lugbak*. *Lugbak* consists of a piece of white cloth with a coin, is delivered by the boys relative to the girl's parents. The father will perform the traditional singing of the *sala* to the girls house in the form of love song to show his intent of acceptance for negotiation. The *sala* of the guy's father also meant observation towards the girl's behavior and her family. It is also the right time for the girl's family to notice the real intent of the guy's father whom he made the *sala*. The girl's parents however, will respond positively by reciting the *sala*. In this *sala* the girl's father will indicate his response. A negative response to girl's parents will be indicated by returning the *lugbak* (white cloth) in a *kagon*. *Kagon* refers to a needle in a cloth which symbolizes non-acceptance. The obligation of setting dowry to the girl's parent's is known as *batang sa bansah*. The traditional dowry is either a piece of land and a carabao. With the advent of Spanish colonization in the Philippines during the sixteenth century, a piece of metal and money is added as a modern system of dowry giving but the traditional way of marriage practices is also carried in today's Higaonon lifestyle).

Bae Daranda shared that *"ang selebrasyon sa kasal gitunong sa maong paagi. Sa atubangan sa balay sa babaye ang kalipay gisugdan sa kalakin-an. Ang babaye nagasul-ob sa kinulintang tinalabi. Ang naandan gihimo aron paghatag sa kalisod sa lalaki sa iyang pagkuha sa babaye. Ang lalaki obligado sa paghatag sa pipila ka kantidad ngadto sa mga parente sa babaye. Ang pagminyo mahimo kana sa pagritwal sa baylan sa ritwal Ang pagbinaylo-ay sa gugma giubanan kini sa inumon nga kan-on nga magsimbolo sa grasya. Ang mama ug tabako usapun aron adunay sandugo sa pamilya"* (the occasion of the wedding day that is a festivity is set for the purpose. In the frontyard of the girl's house, an entertainment is presented by the groom's relative, this is to add attraction and happiness on the wedding day. The bride wears a tribal attire with seven colors of both surrounding the bride in silhouette attraction. This tradition is set to add difficulty on the guy's search for his bride. The groom on his way to the bride's room is oblige to give certain amount for the relatives in the doorstep. That is known as *gandawali*, meaning bridewealth. The vows is to be made in the presence of the *baylan sa ritwal*, the parents and relatives of both sides. The exchange of vows is accompanied by eating the molded rice signifying blessing and graces. The chewing of the betel nuts and tobacco leaves by the couple as well as their parents symbolizes cordiality because of the acquaintances of both families).

Another social activity, that form part of the Higaonon traditional system, is their annual festivity called *Kaamulan*. *"Ang tinuig nga selebrasyon mao ang pagpasalamat, kalipay ug pakig-ambitay sa bag-ong pagkita ug dugang pa nga selebrasyon sa batbat sa istorya kanamong mga Higaonon hilabina sa among katigulangan"*. (the annual celebration is set for thanksgiving, rejoicing, sharing and renewal of acquaintances and above all the festivity is set for tracing the history of our ancestors). The Higaonons believe that during this celebration their ancestor will visit them. The traditional ritual is made in the foothills of the sacred mountains were the *kumba* is located. When the Americans introduced the establishment of a barangay hall, the Higaonons started to have a decorated stage with table known as *talapnay* instead of going the *kumba*. This serves as the central ritual of the Higaonons during their annual *Kaamulan* festivity. They believed that, the supreme god or the magbabaya radiates his power in this *talapnay* where the offering of the Higaonons are made. In this instance, the customary law of their ancestors are revealed to the public spectators.

Adlaw sa gimukod is celebrated in commemoration of their dead ancestors. It is set every second day of November which is an indication of Spanish influence. The offerings are done in the Higaonon cemetery located at the foothills of *Mt. Gabunan*. The offering were consisted of a plate of rice, a cup of wine and betel nuts. These preparations were offered to glorify the spirits of their dead ancestors.

The *Panalikot* features the Higaonon activities at the forest. In the occasion the person who intends to venture the area for hunting purposes may ask to *Diwata Kahungko sa Lasang* for protection against the harmful elementals. The hunting time is dependent on a baylan's dream of abundant food in the community so that when a hunting was done, the spirits could provide him with a caught. Another sign of starting the *panalikot* is during the appearance of a full moon in the sky which signifies the start of the activity. The tradition of ritual in the forest is done by offering betel nut for blessings.

The *Pinag-aso* or *Pista sa Balite* is done quarterly. A *pinag-aso* in December of 2000 was well attended by baylans, datus and farmers. This activity was made a thanksgiving ceremony for protection against harm. The baylans offered his long prayers in the form of latin sayings which is all about thanksgiving and protection. Five chickens, betel nuts and coins were offered near the trunk of a balite tree. This celebration is done to ensure that the *padedeng* will not harm the farmers whose farmlots are located near the balite trees.

The *Pista sa Tubig* is a celebration among the Higaonon fishermen and those people living near the river banks for thanksgiving and more blessings from *Bulalakaw*. This activity was done through a fluvial parade with the use of raft floating at Bayog river. One of this raft was used for setting their offerings which consisted of a live chicken, betel nuts and rice. The occasion was attended by the baylans who led the ritual and some Higaonons who wish to offer their thanksgiving or simply witness the occasion.

Finally, the Higaonons of Rogongon has a tradition that is highly practice. This celebration was known to them as *Alamo*. *Alamo* is an acquaintance of meeting friends and relatives who came from far places. This is significant because it brought renewal of friendship and tribal identity. The activity was done through merrymaking, drinking and relating tribal history of their ancestor.

Kinship Pattern

Datu Bubong Luciano Pianza, a tribal historian, related *"Ang pamilya kanamong mga Higaonon mao kini ang una nga pinaka-importante nga sumbanan. Kini naglangkob sa mga anak ug sa among katigulangan nga nagpuyo sa usa ka balay. Ang amahan mao ang masunod isip lider sa pamilya ug ang pinaka-disiplinado sa tanan"* (the importance of the family as the basic unit in our community. It is an extended family where married siblings live in one dwelling. It is patriarchal in nature where the father is the head of the family and the sole disciplinarian). Jocano (1998) explained that the basic unit of the Philippine society is the family where parents and children provide harmonious relationship. Unlike the society's standard, Pianza further stated that *"ang pag-uso sa upat ka asawa isip usa ang bana gidawat kini sa komunidad. Kana kon ang bana makahatag ug kuwarta uban sa paghigugma sa iyang mga asawa. Ang unang asawa mopuyo usab diha sa usa ka balay"* (the Higaonon practice plural marriages or polygamy among the males only. The husband is allowed to have at most four wives as long as he can equally share the wives with care and financial support. The wives live in the same dwellings). According to Bae Teresita So-ong, *"kon ang unang asawa miabot sa edad nga 40 o magulang pa niana, ang bana mangita na ug mas batan-on pa. Ang unang asawa maga-alima na lang sa ilang mga anak"* (when the first wife reaches the age of forty or older, the husband will find a younger woman and the older wife focuses on the upbringing of their children). The Higaonons believe that *"balaanon kayo ang pagsanay"* (procreation is sacred). Datu Bubong shared the concept of child rearing that their children are assets in the family and are necessary to increase their tribal population. He added that he has more than forty children in his three wives. The customary naming of children is followed from parents as a assign of respect. A Higaonon son must take the first name of his father while the daughter take the first name of her mother. The father is called *Amay* and the mother *Inay*.

The Higaonon as stated by Datu Eladio Sangkuan has a common philosophy that *"Ginagawa ko yalan aron maghiusa ta"* (Loves begets unity for all of us). This guiding principle develops the Higaonon's strong unity in their tribe.

Layton as quoted by Levi Strauss (1990) wrote that "kinship, symbolic communication and indigenous classifications of the natural world. The system of the Higaonon kinship is generally the same to the world in general but certain features of their system like the accepted polygamy made them distinct from the majority".

Value System

The Higaonons of Rogongon set number one priority on the preservation of their traditional culture, which is based on customary law. According to Datu Gunzi *"among gi-amoma ang kalinaw sa among komunidad ug isip ka tribung Higaonon. Ang pagtahud sa mga ginikanan ug katigulangan, ang pagrespeto sa among tribu, sa kinaiyahan ug sa katawhan, ang paghinatagay sa pagkaon ngadto sa nagkinahanglan labi sa among abut, ang kayo sa matag usa kanamo labi na sa maayong gawi, ang pagkamatinud-anon sa among prinsipyo labi na sa kustombre, ang paghigugma sa isig katawo ug ang pagkamatinuoron sa among gawi"* (we value peace in our community, obedience to our parents and elders, respect to our tribe, among people and nature, sharing of food specially for those in need, kindness to everyone of us, truthfulness to our principle, love one another and compassion in our attitude).

Moreover, Sergio Alivio shared about their customary law *"ang kinaagi nako sa malumong pagrespeto nga kon adunay tigulang nga nagdala ug bakat sa iyang abot sama sa utanon ug lagutmon, ang batan-on gikinahanglan sa pag-alsa niana, kay kun dili morespeto ang batan-on siya pagahusgahan sa espiritu sa among katigulangan"* (my experience on the value of respect is that when I meet an old man carrying a load of harvest like rootcrops and vegetables, it is the young man's obligation to carry the load by himself because if he will not respect the old man, he may be cursed by his dead ancestors). Kindness and respect to elders is important because the blessings start from the parents. Respect in the entrance of one's home is also governed by rules. If one's door is close, it signifies non-entry. If one finds out that the door is open, only his right foot can step the ladder. This is one way of respecting the right of one's property. The informants added that the reason for this rule is due to the open type of homes among the Higaonons prior to the Christian settlement in Rogongon. It reveals hospitality, signifying that their homes are open to everybody. However, due to Spanish and American architectural designs, they now have walls on their houses for protection purposes.

The concept of peace and resolving conflicts among the Higaonon is governed through their customary law known as *Tampuda hu Balagun* or the Treaty of the Green Vine. Cutting of vine is a symbolic act of cutting feuds. *Tampuda*, according to oral traditions of the Higaonons is re-enacted whenever feuds arise between groups.

Material Culture and World View

Material Culture refers to the pattern of behavior as practice by the group of people in reference to their architectural designs. However, World View refers to the Higaonon perception of mental pictures from the standpoint of their community and cultural practices in relation to the general standard of laws and scientific explanations.

The Higaonon system of belief's recognize both material and non-material culture left as legacy from their ancestors. The Higaonons of Rogongon headed by Onos Daranda identify those material objects as significant contribution to their traditional beliefs an practices. Added to the material culture of the Higaonons is the architectural pattern of their native houses that reflects simplicity. The Higaonon native houses as shared by Mario Salahay *"ang among balay gihimo nga kwadrado gikan sa cogon nga sagbot ug wala kini bungbong"* (the Higaonon homes were built simply in a quadrangular form usually made up of cogon grass and without board or wall as protection). Datu Bubong shared that *"ang klase sa among panimalay nagaparehas usab sa kayano sa among kasing-kasing ug abli sa tanang lumolupyo"* (our simple type of houses reflect our kind and simple nature, and is open for everyone in the community).

Morga as quoted by Agoncillo (1990), described the Philippine native houses before the Spanish conquest. "The houses and dwellings of all these natives are universally set upon stakes *arugues* high above the ground and roof with palm leaves. Among the Higaonon homes, the roof are those of the cogon grass with four to eight pillars or *arugues* but they differ only with having no walls prior to the Spanish regime. Today's homes are indicative of change in terms of structure as a result of Christian migrants. Moreover, the Christian settler as a product of Western influences copied those of Spanish and American structure of homes. The design of these houses are of colonial type that is a square wooden or concrete building, large pillar rooted in the ground and a roof made up of a galvanized materials.

Moreover, the Higaonons in Rogongon were able to establish their own mindset towards the universe. They conceptualize that their customary law is the general standard. Their law provides belief system that is practice since time immemorial. Datu Pianza shared that *"ang among kinabuhi nagalangkob sa buhi ug sa mga kalibutanong espiritu. Among giila ang magbabaya nga maoy tinubdan sa gahom paingon sa langit. Ug usab nagatoo kami nga ang manlulunda moy nagbantay sa kahoy, suba, bato ug busay. Kada usa niining espiritu adunay katungod isip magbalantay sa among trabaho ug panginabuhian"* (our lives are entertwined with the living and the world of the spirits and even with our dead ancestors. We consider the superbeing and the spirits as the source of power who are in charge of the nature like trees, rivers, rocks, mountains and falls. Each of these spirits has their own spheres of influences as the source of protection in our activities. We believe on the influence of our dead ancestors who oversee and bestow blessings upon us). Datu Sangkuan shared about *"ang kultura sa kalinaw sa kalibutan nagasugod sa pagsinabtanay sa gamay nga hugpong sa tawo"* (the culture of world peace starts from the understanding within the small group). Datu Bubong on the other hand shared that *"ang kultura sa kalinaw sa kalibutan makab-ot pinaagi usab sa pagsunod sa naandan nga sistema sama sa pagkamatinud-anon, pagkamaayo ug ang pagrespeto sa gasa sa kinaiyahan"* (the culture of world peace is attainable through the constant practice of our traditional values like honesty, kindness and valuing the gift of nature).

CHAPTER 6

Social Factors and the Higaonon traditional beliefs

Social Factors

Social Factors	Effects to the Higaonon Traditional Beliefs
1. Intoduction of educational system	It facilitated learning of the basic education among the children The system did not change the outlook on customary laws The young adopted the textbook as a system of instruction than in their customary ways of learning
2. Health Programs	The basic medical health programs were introduced The traditional system of curing still practiced despite the advent of modern science
3. Peace Process	The OPAPP, BUF, ECID sponsored conference which enabled the Indigenous people's participation for peace process
4. Religious Ideologies	Christian doctrine, Seventh Day Adventist, "tultul" and Islam brought new religious ideas Oral tradition and the belief on superbeing and the lesser beings still practiced by the majority despite the presence of new religions

5. Interaction patterns between the Higaonons and the lowlanders	Christian migrants reached Rogongon for settlements and farming purposes brought acculturation of: 1. the concept of private ownership is motivated by the logging concessionaires 2. the adoption of visayan dialect, behavior and taste was influenced by the lowlanders

The social factors which contributed to the changes of the Higaonon traditional beliefs include 1.) the introduction of educational system 2.) health programs 3.) peace process 4.) religious ideologies 5.) interaction patterns between the natives of Rogongon and the lowlanders.

Educational System

Section 30 of Republic Act 8371 provides that, "the state shall provide equal access to various cultural opportunities to the Indigenous People through public or private cultural entities, scholarship grants and other incentives".

Gowing (1987) discussed that the Americans sponsored free public education during the American regime from 1913-1920 in Mindanao but it did not reach Rogongon at that time. Kagawad Abungan said that it was only in 1968 during the Marcos regime were roads going to Rogongon were passable because of logging concessionaires. Barangay Captain Roberto So-ong shared that *"ang unang hut-ong nga eskwelahan sa Rogongon naabri niadtong tuig 1970 diin adunay bainte (20) ka mga bata. Ang ekuwelahan gipangunahan ni Mrs. Abungan sa Kalamalamahan"* (primary school in Rogongon with grade one was opened in 1970 starting with twenty (20) pupils. The enrolment was motivated by Mrs. Abungan who was the first teacher of Kalamalamahan Primary School). The school is located five meters from the barangay Poblacion. According to Kagawad Abungan, *"Ang akong asawa maoy naka-aghat sa mga ginikanan aron maka-eskwela ang mga bata"* (my wife took the responsibility of encouraging the parents for the education of their children). The aim of that school system according to residents was *"aron masayon ang pagtuon sa mga bata, ginaulohan kini sa pagtudlo sa naandang kultura"* (to facilitate learning, the teacher teaches the children on the basic values related to their traditional culture). The classes were conducted in visayan language because the students had difficulty in understanding the lessons. The lessons included basic reading and writing until core subjects were ready to be introduced. Among the original twenty

(20) pupils of 1970 only ten (10) graduated but there was an increase of enrollees with additional number of teachers. The edifice made up of wood was its additional development. The teaching was based on liberal orientation, it has no signs of religious indoctrination such as Catholicism. The introduction of public school system did not change the customary laws among the Higaonons.

A high school teacher shared that, *"ang ika-duhang hut-ong sa eskwela gitukod niadtong tuig 1976 ug adunay unom (6) ka estudyante nga kabahin adtong tuig 1982"*. (secondary school was established in 1976 with six (6) students following the general public education system. Six (6) students graduated in 1982 from the Secondary level). The educational system in Rogongon did not change the outlook of the old folks but the students who exhibited more time in schools imitated western viewpoints particularly that of american thinking and reasoning. Their oral tradition such as oral history, songs and system of belief that contained in their *gitamod* as the non-formal education system became of secondary importance.

Health Programs

The City Government of Iligan in cooperation with the City Health Office extended their outreach health programs and facilities to barangay Rogongon since 1980. A small clinic was constructed at Rogongon proper to facilitate the medical needs of the people. According to the traditional midwives assigned in the clinic they said that basic medical and health programs such as monthly physical and dental examination was instituted. Dr. Abner Villarin headed the medical team with five (5) nurses but the team only visits the barangay once a month. Aside from the medical team assigned, four (4) Higaonon volunteers extended assistance at the barangay clinic. These medical assistants were the traditional midwives namely: Maria Degumbis, Erlinda Cunto, Palermo Guicanan and Uldarica Aranas. They were those engaged in *"hilot"* who assisted the pregnant women in their delivery. Maria Degumbis shared that they volunteered to work in the clinic for further knowledge in modern science. The traditional midwives exhibited their work more than a midwife because they acted as "clinic nurses" in the absence of the medical teams. In fact they prescribed medicines to simple ailments such as headache, stomachache, diarrhea and other common ailments. Datu Cunto shared that *"kami motultul sa among masakiton ngadto sa klinika ug makabalo sa mga hinungdan sa sakit sama sa sakit sa panit, pagsuka-suka, labad sa ulo ug buyag sa engkanto. Apan ang naanadan nga pag-alim sa mga sakit nagpadayon gihapon. Kami nagatuo sa panambal sa baylan sama sa tawal ug yamyam"* (we refer our ailments to the clinic and learn some of the causes of illness but the Higaonon traditional beliefs persisted to the solution for about all kinds of ailments ranging from skin diseases, vomiting, headache which we call discomfort. We believe in the cure of saliva and yamyam). *Yamyam* is a form of healing with the use of "latin" language being expressed by the baylans towards the patient. These are words from the diwata that are chanelled through the baylans. A farmer named Onos Daranda suffered an incident of severe headache. He felt the pain after upon his arrival at his residents. He remembered that he forgot to offer a ritual of permission of entry in his newly opened farm one hundred fifty meters from his farmlot. He then called Baylan Kaamuran to perform the healing ritual. The baylan uttered a word in Latin and touch the affected part of the patient by his finger with his own saliva. He touched the patients head for almost thirty minutes, fortunately the pain suffered by him disappeared and turned normal. The use of *yamyam* as a traditional healing method added a kind of ritual efficacy, that is a power to produce a healing effect immediately particularly an ailments related to *buyag* as shared by the baylans. The accessibility of modern medicines never changed the Higaonon belief on the power of the baylans ritual. The Higaonons of Rogongon still went through the nearest baylan healer if there is a physical discomfort in them. They expressed that *"ang among sakit kasagaran gisugdan sa buyag sa padedeng kon makalimot kami sa pagrespeto ilabina sa balite. Ang mga kuyaw nga lugar sama sa pangpang maoy ilang puloy-anan"* (our sickness are primarily caused by the cursed of the *padedeng* if anyone failed to respect their existence especially that on of the balite trees, the rare places and isolated sites known to be the abode of these elementals).

Moreover, the Higaonons of Rogongon did not agree in the introduction of birth control. The medical teams from the City of Iligan went to Rogongon because of their annual campaign of population control. The team introduced birth contraceptives such as Pills, IUD and condom. Datu Luciano, a tribal historian shared *"ang pagsanay kanamong mga Higaonon, mao ang sagrado nga butang kay gasa kana gikan sa magbabaya mao nga dili gayod namo supakon"* (procreation is sacred and is a natural gift from the magbabaya. Therefore it must not be altered nor bypassed). Datu Luciano further shared that *"ang pagsanay importante gayod tungod kay kaming mga Higaonon sa Rogongon gusto magpabilin sa among tribo"* (procreation is important to us because we want to preserve our tribe). The National

Statistics Office's records of Iligan City showed the population growth of Rogongon from 2,000 in 1970 and 5,000 in 1990. The population growth of Rogongon was based on the decision of the elders on the preservation of the Higaonon tribal population because procreation to them is sacred. Moreover, the elders particularly the datus had observed the contribution of children as asses to their agricultural activity such that children could help their parents in the farm. The practice of steady growth of population in Rogongon would mean a failure to the medical teams in their campaign of birth control. Consequently, the idea of procreation as sacred among the Higaonons of Rogongon is an indication of preserving their traditional beliefs system instead of modern health methods.

Another health measures in Rogongon is directed to water facilities, Datu Guicanan in an interview said *"ang dakong problema mahitungod unsaon paglimpyo sa tubig nga ilimnon aron adunay hapsay nga pagbati sa matag kinabuhi"* (cited major concerns on the immediate installation for a sanitary potable drinking water to improve the healthful conditions of life). Moreover, Datu Dimapinggun stated that, *"ang gisugdan nga programa sa pagtaod sa tubig aduna na, apan kulang ang panudlanan sa lokal na gobyerno"* (the propose program for the water installation is ready, but it needs implementation from the city government of Iligan as soon as funds is appropriate).

Peace Process

Datu Rogelio Cabiladas and Sultan Mama Komunog were the Higaonon representatives for a wider Mindanao forum for peace. One example of their attendance was that of *A Research Training on Indigenous People Belief System: Its Implication to the Peace Process* held in Samal Island, Davao City. The concept on peace process, tribal culture and system of beliefs were those major topics of concerned. The concepts were extended in the community of Rogongon thru a re-echo seminar for the awareness of the Higaonon populace about Mindanao development for peace. Cabiladas shared that the results of the re-echo seminar did not change the existing traditional beliefs such as the recognition of supernaturals among the Higaonon. Instead it gave them wider knowledge for peace. Morino Lihayan shared that, *"ang naandan nga pagtoo ug kustombre nagpalig-on sa among pagsabot sa among tribung balaod"* (the traditional beliefs on customary law and oral tradition were strengthened by understanding the laws of the Indigenous People). In fact the concepts promoted during the conference was geared towards the respect of the Indigenous People traditional belief as a basic operation of peace process.

Datu Macadatar So-ong narrated that *"niadtong tuig 1989 ang Katoliko mikaylap dinhi sa Rogongon ug nagtudlo kanamo sa napulo ka sugo sa Ginoo"* (in the year 1989, the Catholic doctrine reached Rogongon and it taught us the Ten Commandments of God). Teresita Daranda shared that *"ang pagkaylap sa Kristohanong sistema nahimo tungod sa mga sacristan nga misaka dinhi gikan sa Iliganon pagsangyaw sa bibliya niadtong tuig 1989"* (the introduction of Christian system was motivated by the lay ministers of Iligan City Parish sometime in 1989 to evangelize the natives of Rogongon). One way of introducing the faith was through the recruitment of the young male Higaonon age 15-20 to be part of the Catholic movements to serve as *sacristan*. Datu Eladio Sangkuan shared his experiences as one of the sacristan in the Parish of Iligan City. According to him, *"ako nagsilbi sa simbahan ug nakita nako nga ang pagtudlo sa Katoliko pareha sa kaayuhan walay kalainan sa among kustombre"* (I served as a sacristan in the parish church and studied the gospel and found out that the values taught in the church are the same as to what our customary law taught us). The tangible development of Catholicism is manifested through the construction of Catholic chapel with Santo Niño as patron Saint. Significant to note however, is that only a small number of Christians in Rogongon are practicing the Catholic faith. The Higaonon of Rogongon however observed that *"ang sistema sa Kristohanong pugtuo dinhi sa Rogongon wala nakausab sa among naandan nga pagtoo sama sa paghalad ngadto kang magbabaya, sa manlulunda ug sa mga espiritu sa among katigulangan, gani ang Kristiyano nakadugang sa among paghuna-huna sa pagka-matinudanon"* (the system of Christianity did not change our traditional belief like for instance the ritual and offering to our superbeing, lesser beings and dead ancestors. Our observation of the Christian practices only added points of reflection in our values like honesty).

Seventh Day Adventist on the other hand was brought and influenced by Datu Sangkuan to Rogongon who was a former converts of this religion out of his curiosity to know about biblical teachings. Datu Sangkuan had been for three years as an Adventist in Iligan City. When he returned to Rogongon early in the 1970 he preached the doctrine to his relatives and converted them. However, this religion did not strengthen their faith but find comparisons to traditional belief. According to him, *"kontento nako sa akong nakita ug napraktis nga kustombre tungod sa kagawasan sumala sa mando sa among naandan kang magbabaya ug sa mga espiritu"* (I only find contentment and freedom in the customary laws through personal contact with god and spirits). Kagawad Dimapinggun stressed that, *ang among pagtuo sa gitamod maoy nakahatag sa kanunay nga pagtuo ngadto kang magbabaya*" (our faith is strengthened in our customary law that is a practical explanation on the existence of god). A practical explanation according to him "*dali nga solusyon sa problema ginabasa sa pulong sa gitamod*" (an immediate solution of problems that is based on customary law).

Kagawad Timbangan shared his experience as well. According to him, "*ako usa ka tultul nga nagtuon sa bibliya apan gibalhin kini labi na sa mga pulong ngadto sa binukid nga sinultihan. Ang nakadeperinsya lang tungod nga ang mga tultul dili mosimba sa kapilya sa mga Katoliko*" (I am a person who studies the bible and translates it to the vernacular. The only difference is that we do not eat meat and do not manifest our belief by going to church or attend masses). Only few follow the system, in fact Kagawad Timbangan said that "*ako maoy pinakamatinud-anon nga nagtuman sa kustombre bisan ug nakatuon na ako ug bibliya*" (I am still a full pledge believer of the customary laws even with the biblical knowledge that I had studied).

According to Kaamuran Daranda, "*ang pagkaylap sa Islam nga pagtuo niabot dinhi sa Rogongon sukad pa kami nakatimaan ug buot niining lugara kay silingan lang kini sa Lanao del Sur apan gipalambo gihapon ang pagsunod sa pagtuo ngadto lang magbabaya ug sa ubang espiritu sama sa paghalad tungod kay kini kabubut-on lang namo kaysa muhatag kami ug kuwarta sama sa ubang pagtuo*" (the Islamic influence came into the Higaonon community ever since we remembered our existence in this place because of the geographical nearness of Rogongon to Lanao del Sur. With observation he found out that the belief in nature is natural and does not demand any form of tithes, only practical offerings).

Tuante (1998) in his study on the *Early People of Bayug* claimed that, the intermarriages between the Christians and the Muslims are indicated by the Maranao roots of Iligan illustrados who administered the town during the American colonial regime". Intermarriages between these people significantly resulted to interaction patterns of mixed ancestry.

Interaction patterns between the Higaonons and the lowlanders

Malinowski as quoted by Gloria (1987) advocates that the study of social change is diverted to the impact of high culture and the interaction between the native and the Christian resulted into impact and acculturation.

The process of acculturation among the Higaonons was more of the social conditions that were influenced by migrants' ang loggers.

The oral tradition of the Higaonons as shared by Datu Bubong, a tribal historian who claimed that the Higaonons were the first settlers of the coast particularly that of Bayug Island, where the junction of Bayog river is located. Tuante (1998), in his study on the *Early People of Bayug* claimed that the Higaonons and other Maranaos were the first to settle in Bayug island before the Spanish period. Bayug island is located 3.5 kilometers Northeast of Iligan City. Tuante further stated that in 1625 the Agustinian recollects headed by Fray Juan de Nicolas established his mission, which resulted by some natives to move towards the interior of the mountain. The main reason for their transfer of settlement could be attributed to their value system. In an interview with Datu Bubong, he said that, *"ang kaayo namong mga Higaonon nagsumikad pa sukad na sukad"* (kindness among the Higaonons were practice since time immemorial). He reiterated that *"kami dali dayon mobalhin sa among pinuy-anan hangtod ngadto sa kabukiran para lang sa mga bag-ong nangabot nga katawhan dinhi sa Mindanao"* (we are willing to vacate in the hinterland for the benefit of the new comers in Mindanao). Another change in the Higaonon lifestyle was indicative during the arrival of logging concessionaires in 1968 to Rogongon. The arrival of loggers contributed in the accessibility of transportation for the people in Rogongon in going to Iligan City. However, Eliseo Salahay recalled that, *"ang among sagradong lugar madisturbo tungod sa pag-guba sa mga negosyante sa kahoy"* (our sacred sites were disturbed due to the distruction caused by logging business). Datu Eladio said that *"kung kami mangutana sa ilang pag-abot duhulan lang dayon kami ug papeles nga pinirmahan sa mga dagkong tawo alang sa ilang seguridad para makaputol ug kahoy sa kaugalingon nilang negosyo"* (when we questioned their appearances in the area, a validated paper signed by authorities was shown to us on their right to cut trees for their own business). The disturbances in sacred sites caused by the loggers did not change the Higaonon's reverence towards nature. The advent of logging company in Rogongon resulted to signs of social interaction which is evident in their adoption of the visayan language, style of clothing and even food.

CHAPTER 7

SUMMARY and CONCLUSION

The writing on local history is indeed a humble contribution to Philippine Literature. The ethnohistory of the Higaonon tribe will enable the people to understand the grassroots of their distinct culture. Their beliefs, values, attitudes and experiences underwent the process of change attributed to the western policies in the Philippines. The Spanish policy for instance, gave a new system of ideas that only the influential people and the political elite would participate.

However, the native people from the different provinces of the country remained silent and are not included in the mainstream of civilization for they are mainly Manila-centered activities. In this regard, the authors like Mojares, Gloria, Sonza, Agoncillo and others gave an explanation on the importance of local studies to re-orient the focus to the mass-based populace. Although the natives of Rogongon adopted changes, it was still proportionate to the Higaonon's respect towards their belief system. Finally, it is significant to note that despite the advent of civilization, they retain their traditional behavior. Their folklore is worth to be documented in view of Philippine ethnohistory.

There were forty-two (42) respondents in this study. They were chosen purposively from the tribal settlements of Rogongon. Following a purposive non-probability sampling procedure. Two (2) key informants represented the Higaonon baylans, ten (10) were from the Higaonon datus, ten (10) from the Higaonon senior citizens. The methods of data gathering include 1.) fieldwork and participatory observation 2.) personal interviews and focused group discussion 3.) Archival and library research as Higaonons respect the power of the elementals like the *padedeng* and *engkanto* whose abode were identified to be found in the *awa-aw* or isolated and risky places sometimes impassable by humans. The spirits of the Higaonon ancestors are revered because of their historical contributions in the making of the Higaonon oral history. The following are the names of their ancestors *Apo Agyo, Apo Sominam-ang kon Tominokol, Apo Palatambul su Palakampana, Apo Nangadon, Apo Insayan, Apo Nabanglisan, Apo Mangawan, Apo Migsuanob, Apo Imbalagil, Apo Makaupaw, Apo Balingbingan, Apo Banlag, Apo Amantaw-antaw, Apo Dalinason, Apo Pamulaw and Apo Magbabasuk*. Finally, the Higaonons also revere *balaang butang* known to be those inanimate objects considered to be significant because of its value as inheritance. The following are the inanimate objects: *gantangan pandaut sulutan,* weighing scale for peacepact. It symbolizes accuracy. *Bangkaw,* sword symbolizes bravery among the Higaonon ancestor in their hunting purposes.

The origin of the name Rogongon is attached to the term *logong,* meaning a strong wind that presses the contact of tropical trees into a huge sound like thunder. The Limunsudan falls added legends and mythical story of Rogongon aside from being one of the major attraction in the area for it is attributed as *pultahan sa langit* meaning the gateway to heaven and is the home of the *manlulunda* and the place where *Apo Agyo* and *Apo Sominam-ang kon Tominokol* were blessed.

The origin of the Higaonon in Rogongon is believed to be the descendants of *Apo Sominam-ang kon Tominokol* and *Apo Agyo*. *Apo Sominam-ang kon Tominokol's* story could be traced back from the event of a great flood. *Apo Sominam-ang kon Tominokol* was mandated by an angel to trace the origin of the Bayog river until he reached the source of the falls and right there he was blessed by the spirits in Limunsudan falls. *Apo Agyo* on the other hand, was blessed by the spirits of Limunsudan falls. He believed to be a remarkable person among the Higaonons of Butuan, Cagayan, Tagoloan and Bayog since he was the chieftain of those places and he ruled the kingdom. From Butuan where he originated, he was *gibayog,* meaning blown by the wind, and reaches the junction of the Bayog river during the fourteenth century.

The *Ulaging, Sala* and the *Darinday* are the myths which were established based on customary law among the Higaonons of Rogongon. The *Ulaging* refers to an account of stories and genealogies of *Apo Agyo* in the form of a poem; the *sala* refers a song that is chanted on occasion of courtship and marriage festivities. *Darinday* is sang during thanksgiving and acquaintances.

The geographical, historical and even religious considerations of the Higaonons of Rogongon could be attributed to the recognition of their sacred landmarks and sites. These places were included in the oral tradition of the Higaonon like the following mountains: *Mt. Tambulan, Mt. Ligui, Mt. Dungguan, Mt. Kalatungan, Mt. Tominokas and Mt. Piloasan.*

Section 23 of Republic Act 8371 provides the Indigenous Peoples right to their ancestral sites, significantly, the baylans and datus through their oral tradition encourage the Higaonons to properly respect and recognize these places. A manifestation of the Higaonons' respect is evident in their adherence of ancestor worship—that is referring to their dead ancestor's blessedness and immortality that historically happened in that place. In this regard, the Higaonons offer ritual each time they wish to venture the area. In addition, is the significance of the *kumba* which is referred to as the traditional ritual site situated in the heavy forested area of Mt. Tambulan where the ritual of thanksgiving is done. During the American period, when the Higaonon social hall was established, the *kumba* was replaced by the *talapnay. Talapnay* is set in a white cloth with leaves of betel nuts decorated therein and the offering consist of betel nuts, tobacco and coin. It is believed to be the place where the *magbabaya* radiates his power. The *Sagyaan Cave* is important because of the eventual retreat of the Higaonon against their tribal enemy. It is also their ancestor's area for worship. *Limunsudan Falls,* on the other hand, is believed to be the dwelling of the lesser spirits and it is also where the Higaonon ancestors were blessed. The City Planning for Agro Forestry Division of Iligan City implemented in 1995 the identification of these Higaonon landmarks and sites.

The Higaonon social conditions are classified into the aspects on social systems, kinship patterns, value system and material culture and world view. The social social system of the Higaonon is primarily dominated by male as head of the family and of the society. The classification of social status is due to the philosophy of their ancestors that the men should be more superior than women. The qualities of a chieftain should include: fair judgement, honesty and bravery in his leaderhip in the community. Baylan are of two types: the *baylan sa kaligaon* and the *baylan sa ritwal.* The baylans posses powers which are guided by the spirits. He may perform ritual on all occasions like farming, marriages, thanksgiving and even cure ailments by virtue of his power in order to ward off bad elementals. Moreover, kinship pattern revolves around the lineage of father whose family name shall be used by future siblings. The Higaonon family is extended-children and wives live in the same dwelling. The Higaonon however practice polygamy, it is possible fo a man to have four wives as long as he can afford to give them financial support. The Higaonons value obedience, respect, sharing, kindness and truthfulness. These virtues strengthen the idea geared towards peace.

A wider sphere of the Higaonon values will develop a meaningful achievement of peace among Indigenous People, Christian and Muslim. Peace to the Indigenous People is attainable if they be given the right to manifest and practice their traditional beliefs and recognize their system.

The Higaonon's material culture is manifested in the architectural designs of their homes—no walls and made up of cogon grass—signifying simplicity.

The various opportunities of the Indigenous People were specified in Section 30 of Republic Act 8371 providing the natives with socio-cultural accessibility. The Higaonon social factors include the introduction of educational system, health programs, peace process, religious ideologies and interaction patterns.

One evident development in Rogongon is the construction of school building in 1970 with an initial number of twenty pupils and the lone school teacher was Mrs. Abungan, The curriculum was based on western teaching. The construction of the secondary school followed in 1976. Higaonons continue to practice their customary law and tradition while learning the western ideas. Health programs were extended to Rogongon in 1970 when Dr. Abner Villarin and five nurses headed the medical team. The introduction of basic medicines for headache, diarrhea and stomachache never effaced the Higaonons belief on the traditional baylans efficacy and power in healing and curing their ailments. Even snake bites could be cured by *tawal* or saliva curing.

The peace process significantly developed human personality and their respect towards superbeing and the existing nature spirits. Religious ideologies gradually develop curiosity among the natives and even the baylans (like for instance in their affiliation to Catholic doctrine, Seventh Day Adventist, Tultul and Islam) but they only develop the virtues which are also found in their religious beliefs. The Higaonon found out that all belief system regardless of creed are of the same origin, which is, under the presence of God the Father for Christian, Allah for the Muslim and Magbabaya for the Indigenous Peoples. In that event, the Indigenous People finds freedom in their reverence towards superbeing, lesser beings, spirits of their dead ancestor and inanimate objects that are contained in their tradition. The Higaonon's line of thinking is seen through this denomination but it did not alter their traditional system.

The interaction patterns between the Higaonons of Rogongon and the lowlanders significantly develop. The migration of lowlanders during the commonwealth regime to Rogongon and the purchase of lands by the Christians gave views to the Higaonon concept of currency than those of the traditional barter system.

Conclusion

Historical findings of various authors support that Rogongon was a place of settlement among the Higaonons. The influx of migrants in Rogongon during the commonwealth regime (1935-1941) develops certain process of acculturation. This process between the Higaonons of Rogongon and the lowland Christians resulted to intermarriages. Added to the process is the adoption of visayan dialect to the Higaonon system. Manner of dressing, house type and taste of food were among the influences of these new settlers but these did not pose a serious challenge among the Higaonons. The creation of Rogongon into a barangay in 1968 has encouraged a wider political process that eventually developed into the people's concept of democratic participation. One political activity that shaped the justice system was the entrance of the logging concessionaire of Rogongon in 1970's. The logging company provided effect to the Higaonon's concept of communal ownership of land. These conditions such as the migration process and logging business contributed to the development and progress while retaining their customary laws like beliefs and practices.

The strengthening of the Higaonon beliefs were evident in the preservation of their natural resources which served as landmark and heritage that are sacred by reasons of religious or personal advantage. Rogongon could be more productive and profitable aside from the resources inherent in the place by making the place as an eco-tourism village without destroying the environment. The attractions of the place include Limunsudan falls, the legendary Bayog river, the forest reserves, Sagyaan cave and sacred mountains are the pride of the Higaonons which are still at its natural prestine. Having this resources would develop earnings from the Higaonon through any kinds of handicraft such as making baskets out of anotong trees, wood engraving that depicts Higaonon art and earn more by allowing them as tourist guide in the caves or engaged in boat canoeing at bayog river while sightseeing the greenish resources near Limunsudan falls. However, the visitors should also be oriented that visiting sites could be started after the necessary ritual is finished. In this regard the visitors will be able to know the tourist spots but also learning the culture of the Higaonon people which is vital for peace process. Furthermore, the existing tripartite system and the Higaonons' purpose for peaceful co-existence could be attained through the understanding of the real belief and practices of the Higaonon tribe.

GLOSSARY OF HIGAONON TERMS

Alamo—it means shadow. Significantly, the term would mean the presence of shadows during an occasional gathering for a cause of celebration among the Higaonons of Rogongon.

Bae—It refers to a female title of prestige and honor.

—it also means a title of the female Higaonons in Rogongon whose responsibility and function include: community peacemaker, birth attendant, secretary, herbdoctor, teacher and an assistant of a datu or baylan during the ritual process.

Batbat sa Kasaysayan—an oral presentation of history that is completed through wit and wisdom by the leading datus and baylans of Rogongon during Kaamulan festival.

Baylan—Traditionally he has been a datu by virtue of honor (exemplary service) good example and wisdom. He moreover, possess powers from being a prophet *(mubala)*, performed ritual *(mubuhat)* and above all a religious functionary.

Baylan sa ritwal—religious functionary who is guided by spiritual being and is empowered to cure illness caused by the curse of padedeng.

Baylan sa Kaligaon—a tribal leader who led the presentation of their tribal history during Kaamulan festival.

Bayog—the source of Bayog river and the origin of the Limunsudan Falls.

Binukid—refers to the Higaonon native language as vernacular.

Buyag—an illness caused by the harmful elementals.

Darinday—the Higaonon epic song of thanksgiving and acquaintance.

Datu—it refers to a title of distinction and position in the tribal stratification addressed to a person in authority by virtue of wisdom, bravery and seniority.

—similarly in the Higaonon community, a datu is selected by virtue of inheritance.

—He is chosen from his forefather and his relatives in lieu of his potential in dealing with disputes and is gifted with bravery and wisdom. He also inherits knowledge related to tribal history and culture. He can also perform certain ritual on farming, marriage, thanksgiving and others.

Diwata—the good elementals; fairy.

Engkanto—the unforeseen forces of nature like *diwata* and *padedeng*.

Gimukod—the souls of the Higaonon.

Gitamod—refers to an oral history and traditions of the Higaonons in Rogongon which include *sala, darinday* and *malingka*.

Higaonon—as defined in this research work, these are the *tagabukid* or the mountain dwellers who are the major inhabitants of Rogongon.

—it also refers to as dwellers of the hinterland (Rodil, 1998)

Kaamulan—The Higaonons' year-end celebration of thanksgiving that features *legudas* and *kaliga*.

Kagon—a box that contains the needle and a cloth of a denied proposal for marriage.

Kaliga—a festive of relating the Higaonons tribal history during the *Kaamulan* celebration; the baylan contest for wit and wisdom.

Kinulintang Tinalabi—the Higaonon bridal attire which consisted of seven colors.

Kumba—the traditional ritual site held at the forest of Mt. Gabunan.

Lagudas—the merry-making of the Higaonon which features the tribal dances celebrated during the year end *Kaamulan* festival.

Lugbak—white cloth with needle used to deny the purpose for marriage

Manlulunda—the right hand of the *magbabaya*.

Mangangayam—the Higaonon hunter.

Padedeng—usually known as the bad elementals.

Pangilihan—the Higaonon hideout that is usually in the cave, *kumba, baka—baka*.

Pangalas—the start of the Higaonon farming activity which is done by cutting off the bushes and trees for clearing purposes.

Pulong—the oral account that has historical and tribal significance.

Pultahan sa Langit—refers to the entrance of heaven located at the source of Bayog river

Rogongon—refers to the place of settlement among the Higaonon tribal community in Lanao del Norte. It is one of the forty-four (44) barangay of Iligan City. It is located in the mountainous Northeastern portion.

Sala—the Higaonon epic song for courtship and marriage.

Salikot—a rope used to tie wild animals during hunting.

Sandugo—the cordiality of bonding relationship for both families on the occasion of marriage vows.

Talapnay—the place of ritual held at the hall where the white cloth, coconut leaves, betel nuts and other offerings are placed therein.

Tagulambong pandaut sulutan—a weighing scale symbolizing equality and justice used by the council of datus to settle conflict.

Tawal—the traditional Higaonon healing to cure the affected part of the body with the use of the saliva

Tampuda hu balagon—an oath of green vine branch or peace pact. An agreement between parties is usually tested through peace pact to attain justice and peace.

Tilad—the Higaonon offerings consisting of betel nuts, coin and a tobacco placed in a plate.

Ulaging—the Higaonon epic of happiness and acquaintance.

Yam-yam—the traditional Higaonon healing with the use of *latin* words dictated by the *diwata* that is chanelled through the *baylan sa ritwal*. It was then effective for curing *buyag* caused by the cursed of the *padedeng*

Definition of Terms

The following terms are here operationally defined as used in this study.

Animism. Refers to the theory which divides into two great dogmas, first concerning souls of individuals, creatures capable of continued existence after the death or destruction of the body; Second, concerning other spirits, upward to the rank of powerful deities (Taylor, 1958).

Artifact. These are the relics or objects of human happenings like a coin, a ruin, a manuscript and a book (Gottschalk, 1969).

Beliefs. Enunciates a strong held ideas in material and non-material world like the presence of the supernatural thing and objects of unexplained phenomena.

Change. A variety of ways in which relationship are ordered and event are put together which depends upon decision of choice (Firth, 1951).

Similarly it implies some confusion about new situations associated with the problems of adopting new methods as well as difficulties in acceptance of new values (Kiev, 1964).

Continuity. It refers to the persistence of a certain pattern on a psychological means to present disruptive forces from disturbing the equilibrium of the system (Burton, 1982).

Culture. Refers to the complex whole which includes knowledge belief, art, morals, laws, customs and any other capabilities and habits by man as a member of a society (Taylor, 1967).

Customs. Refers to behavior acquired by the Higaonon ancestor in the form of language, beliefs and way of life such as courtship, marriage and death practices.

Customary laws. Refers to a body of written and or unwritten rules, usages, customs and practices traditionally and continually recognized, accepted and observed by respective Indigenous Cultural Communities or Indigenous Peoples. (R.A. No. 8371, p.5)

Elementals. Refers to the forces of nature that is of supernatural phenomenon which are classified into good elementals (diwata) and bad elementals (padedeng).

Epic. Refers to the expression of Higaonon songs as portrayed in a certain time through customs and tradition like courtship as expressed in *sala*, as acquaintances as expressed in *malingka* and festivals as expressed in *ulaging*.

Ethnohistory. A study of the tribal people and their past cultural orientation including their customs, beliefs and practices.

Fieldwork. As used in this study, refers to the science of investigation in the field of ethnohistory. The technique has been applied in Rogongon, a settlement of Higaonon tribal Filipinos. The process consisted of an in-depth and focused group interviews with the researcher's participatory observation in ritual and related rites.

Ideology. Means the Higaonon principles in the practice of their beliefs as to their mental conviction in the manifestation of their belief in the superbeing and other related things.

Kinship pattern. A proposed model of relationship especially by blood or affinity.

Landmark. Refers to the physical feature located within the vicinity of Rogongon like rivers and mountains that were considered as historical sites of legends and stories of Higaonon settlement.

Legends. Means a mythology which expresses sentiments towards the Higaonon place of origin and heritage, or of significant genealogical account.

Material Culture. This refers to the pattern of behavior as practiced by the group of people in reference to their precious things and even architectural designs.

Myth. Recounts historical events which explain the tribal origin and identity of the group of people, that which major doctrines and religious concepts arose (Winick, 1956)

National Commission on Indigenous Peoples (NCIP). Refers to the agency of the government under the Office of the President and which is the primary government agency responsible for the formulation and implementation of policies, plans and programs to recognize, protect and promote the indigenous Cultural Communities or Indigenous Peoples. (R.A. No. 8371 p.5)

Oral Tradition. Reveals the learned customs, folkways, habits, norms and beliefs that is contained in their myth through songs, poems and stories verbally transmitted from one generation to the next.

Practice. It deals with the Higaonon customary activities as a manifestation of their belief system as to rites and rituals as a tribute of respect to their supreme beings.

Rites. It portrays a certain period of time wherein the activity of offerings of food, drinks, betel nuts and tobacco are made on occasion of prayers to magbabaya and asking permission in the entrance to sacred places.

Rituals. It is a practice to prescribe formal behavior with a symbolic and solemn presentation which follows a cultural tradition (Rite of Passage, Vol. 2).

—It is also a ceremony performed on specific occasions for purifications and communal celebrations. It may consist of incantations combined with sacrifices (Sigerist, 1967).

Sacred mountain. Refer to an elevated land area located few kilometers from the Higaonon communities proved to have legends as dwelling place of Superbeing, lesser beings and dead ancestors.

Sacred sites. Refer to a place like mountains, a cave, a river and a rock venerated as holy due to the abode of spirits and dead ancestors.

Sacred Organization. As used in this work, this refers to the group of tribal leadership like the datus, baes, baylans and sultan that strengthen their traditional belief system.

Superbeing. As defined in this study, it refers to as the higher god, the supreme, the overseer and the protector of the universe

Time immemorial. Refers to a period of time when as far back memory can go, certain Indigenous Cultural Communities or Indigenous People are known to be occupied, possessed in the concept of owner and utilized a defined territory devolved to them, by operation of customary law or inherited from their ancestors, in accordance with their customs and traditions. (R.A. No. 8371 p.5)

Traditional Beliefs. These are the old practices which imply that they have certain knowledge or superior evidence for their own scientific, philosophical or religious convictions (Castro, 1998).

Tradition. It refers to the Higaonon practices that are handed down from one generation to another in the form of verbal or oral explanation of a certain knowledge in beliefs and practices, peace, sustainability and social system.

Tribal Communities. A homogenous society identified by a group of people who have continuously lived as community bounded and defined territory, sharing common bonds and language, customs, traditions and other distinctive cultural traits, and who through resistance to the political, social and cultural inroads of colonization became historically differentiated from the majority of the Filipinos (DENR Executive Order No.2 Series of 1993).

Tripartite. Refers to the three peoples of Mindanao, the Muslims, the Christians and the Indigenous Peoples.

World View. It refers to the Higaonon perception and mental pictures from the standpoint of their community and cultural practices in relation to the general standard of scientific laws.

BIBLIOGRAPHY

Books

LOCAL PUBLICATION

Agoncillo, Teodoro A. *History of the Filipino People.* 8th ed. Quezon City: Garotech Publishing, 1990.

Castro, Jovito. *Anthropology of Asean Literature: Epics of the Philippines Asean Commission on Culture and Information.* 1998.

Datu Sandigan sa Bayog et al Fact Sheets. *Sacred History of the Kingdom of Tagoloan.* Tampuda Development Council Inc. 2000.

Demetrio, Francisco R. SJ. *Philippine Myths and Symbols.* Metro Manila: National Bookstore Inc., Revised Edition, 1990.

Demetrio, Francisco R. SJ. *Dictionary of Philippine Folk Beliefs and Customs.* Xavier University: Modern Press, 1970.

Demetrio, Francisco R. SJ. *Illustrated Folktales.* Metro Manila: National Bookstore Inc., Revised edition, 1990.

Enriquez, Antonio R. *Subanon.* Metro Manila: University of the Philippines Press, 1999.

Gloria, Heidi K. *The Bagobos: Their Ethnohistory and Acculturation.* Quezon City: New Day Publishers, 1987.

Jocano, Landa F. *Filipino Indigenous Ethnic Communities Patterns, Variation and Typologies.* Metro Manila: Punlad Publishing House, 1998.

Mercado, Leonardo. *Meeting the Spirituality of the Indigenous Peoples.* Manila: Logos Publication Inc., 1999.

Mercado, Leonardo. *Experiencing the Spirit into the Faith Culture of Kalinga.* Manila: Logos Publication Inc., 1999.

Mercado, Leonardo. *Spirituality on Creation,* Manila: Logos Publication Inc., 1999.

Mojares, Resil. *The Writing of Rural History.* Quezon City: Philippine Social Science Council Publication Inc., 1980.

Nid, Amino. *Filipino Courtship and Marriage Practices Among the Philippine Tribe.* Metro Manila: National Bookstore Inc., 1975.

Rodil, Rudy B. *The Minoritization of the Indigenous Communities of Mindanao and the Sulu Archipelago.* Davao City: Alternate Forum for Research in Mindanao Inc., 1994.

Socio-economic Profile. *Research Evaluation and Statistical Division.* Iligan City, 1991.

Unabia, Carmen C. and Victorino Saway. *Tula at Kwento ng Katutubong Bukidnon.* Quezon City: University of the Philippines Press, 1998.

FOREIGN PUBLICATION

Best, John W. *Research in Education.* 2nd ed. New Jersey: Prentice, 1990.

Blair, Emma H. and Robertson, James Alexander. *The Philippine Islands 1893-1898.* Vol. 39. Cacho Hermanos Inc., 1903.

Cole, Fay-Cooper. *The Bukidnon of Mindanao.* Vol. 46. U.S.A.: Chicago Press, 1956.

Eliade, Mircea. *Myths, Dreams and Mysteries: The Encounter Beween Contemporary Faiths and Archaic Realities.* New York: Harper and Row, 1960.

Gottschalk, Louis. *Understanding History.* New York: Alfred A. Knopf Inc., 1969.

Gowing, Peter. *Heritage and Horizon.* Quezon City: New Day Publishers, 1987.

Hopfe, Lewis M. *Religions of the World.* 3rd ed. New York: McMillan Co. Inc., 1983.

Johnson, John J. *Continuity and Change in Latin America.* California: Stanford University Press, 1964.

Keesing, Edward. *Cultural Anthropology: A Contemporary Perspective.* Cambridge University Press, 1976.

Kroeber, A.L. and Kluckholva, Clyde. *Culture: A Critical Review of Concepts and Definitions.* New York: Alfred A. Knoff Inc., 1952.

Layton, Robert. *An Introduction to the Theory in Anthropology.* U.K. Cambridge University Press, 1997.

Liendhardt, Godfrey. *Social Anthropology.* London: Oxford University Press, 1964.

Livetas, Gloria B. *Culture and Consciousness: Perspective in the Social Science.* New York: George Brazilla, Inc. 1967.

Lowie, Robert H. *Primitive Society.* U.S.A. Liveright Publishing Corporation, 1947.

Mc Null Burns et. al. *World Civilization.* 7th ed. Vol. 1. U.S.A. WW Norton Co. Inc., 1955.

Taylor, Robert. *Cultural Ways: A Compact Introduction to Cultural Anthropology.* New York: White Plains Publication, 1958.

Articles and Unpublished Materials

Absin, Roel. *The History of Laguindingan from 1898-1995.* A Masters Thesis submitted to the Graduate School of Xavier University, 1998.

Basadre, Ma. Corazon, RGS. *Ethnographic Study on the Impact of Modern Farming Techniques in Initao to the Higaonon Traditional Farming.* A paper submitted to Prof. Q. Origenes as a requirement in SOAN 109, Xavier University, 1996.

Binahon Jr., Datu Fundador S. *The Higaonon: National Culture and Arts Contemporary Culture.* Metro Manila: National Commission for Culture and Arts, 1999.

Binahon Jr., Datu Fundador S. *The Higaonon-Southern Cultural Communities.* Metro Manila: National Commission for Culture and Arts, 1999.

Castro, Luz. The Ancestral Domain Claim of the Impahanong—Amusig Tribal Organization: A Study of Higaonon in Malitbog Bukidnon." Indigenous People Apostolate Council Research, Cagayan De Oro City, 1998.

The Baylan-Ulama-Bishop Conference. A Publication Episcopal Commission on Interreligious Dialogue, 1998.

Honda, A. "Comparative Study on the Ifugao and the Manobo Folk Epics in the Light of Religious World View." Masters Thesis, Xavier University, 1996.

Gomez, Ma. Virginia B. *The Higaonons of Imbatug, Bukidnon Way of Life, Past and Present: An Ethnographic Study.* A Paper submitted to Prof. Q. Origines, as a requirement in SOAN 109, Xavier University 1996.

Tuante, Ma. Ines. *The Early History of Bayug.* A Masters Thesis presented to the Department of History Mindanao State University-Marawi, 1998.

Yaptenco, Herminia Q. "Traditional Healing in an Urban Setting in Northern Mindanao: A Study in Change and Continuity." Masters Thesis, Xavier University, 1991.

Other Documents

Department Administrative Order No. 2 series of 1993 *Rules and Regulations for the* Identification Delineation and Recognition of Ancestral Land and Domain Claims.

Third Regular Session. "An Act Recognizing, Protecting and Promoting the Rights of Indigenous Cultural Communities or Indigenous Peoples, creating a National Commission on Indigenous Peoples' establishing, implementing mechanism, appropriating funds therefore and for other purposes".

Resolution No. 155, Series 1962. "On the Creation of Rogongon into a Separate Political Units." An excerpt from the minutes of the regular session of the Municipal of the City of Iligan held at its Session Hall on the 6th day of November, 1962.

Lectures and Conferences

Burton, Erlinda M. "A Study of Culture". A Lecture given during a Conference on a Research Training on the Lumad Belief System, Held at Samal Beach Park, Davao City. November 3-5, 2000.

Sonza, Demy. "A Study on the Western Visayas Placenames." A Paper presented during the 9th National and Local Conference on Local History, held at Bacolod City. October 1980.

www.ingramcontent.com/pod-product-compliance
Lightning Source LLC
Chambersburg PA
CBHW020359290526
45785CB00005B/2359